Drums pound in the distance. Booming war cries and guttural laughter splits the air. The earth shakes under the stomping feet of the monstrous tribes. Run, hide, beg for aid from your weakling gods – it matters not, for the wild warriors of Destruction are on the march, and in their wake they leave behind only rubble and corpses.

From the smallest snotling to the most hulking gargant, these brutish marauders are the children of Gorkamorka, the two-headed god of Ghur, he who is the apex predator of existence and the font of elemental savagery. Fighting and carnage empowers these creatures. They revel in battle and bloodshed, but not to satisfy some notion of holy duty or out of a desire to win favour in the eyes of treacherous deities. These savage warbands fight only to prove themselves the meanest and toughest of their number – and because it fills them with a joy like nothing else.

On some unconscious level, the tribes of Destruction are all driven to return the realms to their most perilously natural state; should they triumph, every realm will be covered by blasted savannahs, frozen tundras and lightless, dank caves. Here, only the strongest and most cunning of predators would thrive, and everything that was once civilised and righteous would be reduced to the status of weakling prey. Might makes right is the creed of Gorkamorka, and his children strive to exemplify this truth with every act of desecration and hooliganism they perform.

Nowhere is safe from the ravages of Destruction, not even the domain of the Everchosen himself. The valleys and mountains of the Bloodwind Spoil ring to the clash of blades as orruks, ogors and grots surge across the land. These are neither the restrained servants of Sigmar nor the mindless puppets of Nagash. Within these creatures burns a core of furious violence that forever aches to be released.

Through raw brutality and instinctive wiles, these belligerent warbands have proven themselves many times over to be equal to the champions of Chaos who claim to rule the Eightpoints. Given time, perhaps they will one day even rise up to challenge the lords of ruin themselves for dominance. On that day, the Bloodwind Spoil will tremble as never before, battered and gouged by an unstoppable onslaught of savage fury.

In the Eightpoints, as in all those places to which Gorkamorka has turned his monstrous gaze, there is only one truth and one law. The strong survive. The weak perish.

SMASH AND BASH!

Roaring and howling, the hordes of Destruction attack in an unstoppable wave of savagery. The monstrous beings that make up their armies fight for the joy of combat – and to please their belligerent deity, the twin-headed god Gorkamorka. Wherever they go, they despoil and defile with abandon, reducing everything in their path to a more primitive state and raucously trampling even the merest hint of civilisation into the dust. When these brutal but cunning creatures go on the rampage, no one is safe.

Warcry: Harbingers of Destruction is the ultimate guide to fighting brutal skirmish battles with the children of Gorkamorka. The wild tribes and monstrous hordes of the Mortal Realms offer an incredibly wide pool of fighters to draw upon; from spiteful grots, dull-witted troggoths and boisterous orruks all the way to ravenous ogors and bellowing gargants, there's no shortage of deadly brutes and marauders ready to rampage and batter their way across the Bloodwind Spoil.

Harbingers of Destruction contains complete rules for fielding Warcry warbands from the hungering Ogor Mawtribes, devious Gloomspite Gitz and rampaging Orruk Warclans. The expansive background offers insights into the history and culture of these factions, as well as the motives and methods that define their battles in the Eightpoints. Ability

cards and full fighter rules will provide you with all the information you need to choose a warband of brutal but cunning (or cunning but brutal, in the case of the vindictive grots) warriors and get right into the thick of the action. Also included are a series of name and background generation tables, helping you to personalise the quirks, origins and identities of your warband and turn every warrior you recruit into an individual and characterful fighter in their own right.

However, there's more to *Harbingers of Destruction* than just the raw rules for mustering and battling with a warband. Four new fated quests have been included that are open to any warband pledged to the cause of Destruction; over the course of these violent adventures, you'll explore many areas of the Bloodwind Spoil and battle against all manner of foes to achieve your goals. The fated quest system allows

The mobs and warbands of Destruction care next to nothing about who they are fighting. As long as the battles are regular and bloody, they will set themselves against anyone unfortunate enough to cross their path.

you to decide the outcome of your campaign – not only does this offer you the chance to truly develop the story and motivations of your own personal warband, but you will also get access to a choice of powerful rewards to make your fighters even more fearsome on the battlefield. In addition, a series of new challenge battles offer bespoke Warcry scenarios themed around the followers of the twin-headed god. Each of these special missions offers a unique trial to overcome; though they can be difficult even for experienced warbands, the benefits – not to mention the bragging rights – gained from mastering them all is something to revel in. Along with expanded rules for supplementing your warband with allies, thralls and monstrous beasts, there's plenty of content to dig into that's sure to satisfy all true devotees of Destruction.

However you choose to enjoy Warcry, be it by playing through exciting narrative campaigns, diving into the fires of competitive play or just creating great and memorable battles with your friends, the most important thing to remember is to have fun, and few warbands are better at promoting this viewpoint than the wild warriors of Destruction!

Every model in the range is infused with personality, and painting them is a great joy in its own right, allowing you to experiment with different textures, tribal markings and warpaint designs. On the battlefield, the sheer brawn and madcap cunning employed by the children of Gorkamorka makes them great fun to play with – whether you choose to overwhelm your enemies with savage might or outwit them with a predator's cunning, you have plenty of options to play your way. Now, get out there and start smashing!

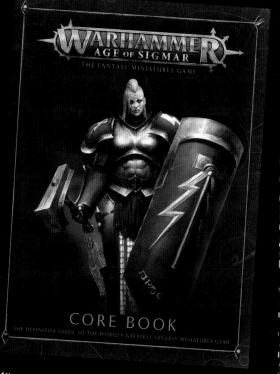

YOUR JOURNEY CONTINUES...

The jaw-dropping expanse of the Eight Realms is all but limitless, and so are the opportunities for exciting games of Warhammer Age of Sigmar.

The Warhammer Age of Sigmar Core Book is your in-depth guide to this fantastical setting. As well as a full and detailed history of the Mortal Realms, from the legendary tales of the Age of Myth to the triumphant crusades of the Stormcast Eternals, you will find a detailed overview of several of the most heavily contested realms. Included within are introductions to each of the Grand Alliances battling across these magical lands, from the tireless legions of Death to the rampaging, howling hordes of Destruction.

Exciting narrative sections, breathtaking world-building and detailed timelines – along with a showcase section presenting beautifully painted Citadel Miniatures in all their glory – will offer plenty of inspiration for your own hobby collection.

Of course, within the pages of the Core Book, you will also find the full core rules for the Warhammer Age of Sigmar tabletop game, laying out each stage of a battle in intuitive and easy-to-follow stages. Whether you wish to take on your friends in a balanced competitive match or prefer to simulate a mythic encounter between fantastical armies in the form of a narrative campaign, this weighty tome provides everything you need to lead your mighty army into battle!

HOW TO USE THIS BOOK

Warcry: Harbingers of Destruction contains all of the rules you need to field the Warcry warbands of Destruction on the battlefields of the Bloodwind Spoil and beyond.

DESTRUCTION WARBANDS

The rules in this book will often refer to **Destruction warbands**. Every warband in Warcry belongs to one of the following 4 Grand Alliances: **Chaos**, **Death**, **Destruction** or **Order**. A Destruction warband is any warband that has one of the faction runemarks listed in the box on the right.

In addition, if any rules have the **Destruction** runemark (☠), those rules apply to all Destruction warbands. For example, the Destruction fated quests in this book all have the **Destruction** runemark (☠) and can only be embarked upon by Destruction warbands.

The rules in this book are split into the following sections:

HEROES AND ALLIES

This section explains how to include heroes and allies in your warband.

MONSTERS AND THRALLS

This section contains rules for using monsters in your Warcry battles, including abilities for fighters to use against monsters and abilities for the monsters to use themselves. There are also rules for including monsters in your warband, plus fighter cards and abilities for the monsters and thralls available to a Destruction warband.

WARBANDS

This section includes all the abilities and fighter cards for Destruction warbands. There are 4 factions available to choose from.

CAMPAIGNS

This section includes 4 Destruction fated quests that any Destruction warband can embark upon.

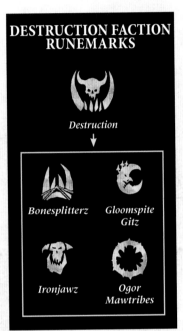

DESTRUCTION FACTION RUNEMARKS

Destruction

↓

Bonesplitterz | *Gloomspite Gitz*

Ironjawz | *Ogor Mawtribes*

CHALLENGE BATTLES

This section contains rules for playing challenge battles and includes 6 challenge battles that any Destruction warband can embark upon.

HEROES AND ALLIES

In the Bloodwind Spoil, each day is a battle for survival. Many warbands seek to make alliances with powerful heroes and champions, for together they stand far greater chance of mastering the wilds than either does alone.

This section provides rules for special types of fighter known as **heroes** and **allies**. These rules allow you to include more than 1 fighter with the **Leader** runemark (☀) in your warband, as well as fighters with a different faction runemark to your warband. This gives you even more ways to theme your warband and make it unique. For example, your Ogor Mawtribes warband might be led by a Tyrant who enlists the skills of an Icebrow Hunter to stalk your prey, or perhaps your Ironjawz have been joined by a mad Wurrgog Prophet.

If you have the *Warcry: Monsters and Mercenaries* expansion, the rules in this section supersede the allies rules in that book.

INCLUDING HEROES AND ALLIES IN YOUR WARBAND

Any fighter with the same faction runemark as your warband and the **Leader** runemark (☀) can be included in your warband as a **hero**.

Any fighter with a different faction runemark to your warband and either the **Leader** runemark (☀) or the **Ally** runemark (◯) can be included in your warband as an **ally**. However, warbands can only include allies from the same Grand Alliance. For example, Destruction warbands can only include allies with a Destruction faction runemark.

There are limits on how many heroes and allies you can include in your warband, depending on the style of game you are playing.

OPEN AND MATCHED PLAY
In open play and matched play, when mustering for a battle, you can include 1 hero or ally in your warband. Heroes and allies cost points just like any other fighter, but allies are ignored for the purposes of the rule that requires all fighters in a warband to share the same faction runemark. In addition, when mustering your warband, heroes and allies are not considered to have the **Leader** runemark (☀).

NARRATIVE PLAY
In narrative play, heroes and allies can be added to your warband roster like any other fighter, either when you are first filling out your warband roster or during the Add and Remove Fighters step of the aftermath sequence.

Your warband roster can include up to 3 heroes or allies in any combination. When adding fighters to your warband roster, heroes and allies are not considered to have the **Leader** runemark (☀) and do not count towards the maximum number of fighters you can add.

When mustering for a campaign battle, you can include 1 hero or ally from your warband roster for every 2 areas of territory your warband has dominated. For example, if you have 5 areas of dominated territory,

you can include up to 2 heroes or allies from your warband roster in your warband for that campaign battle. Heroes and allies cost points just like any other fighter, but allies are ignored for the purposes of the rule that requires all fighters in a warband to share the same faction runemark. In addition, when mustering your warband, heroes and allies are not considered to have the **Leader** runemark (☀).

If your warband can include thralls when mustering for a campaign battle, any heroes or allies you include in your warband do not decrease the number of thralls you can include, and vice versa.

Like other fighters, heroes and allies can receive destiny levels, players must make injury rolls for them and they can bear lesser artefacts. Heroes can bear artefacts of power and be chosen to become favoured warriors, but allies cannot.

HEROES AND ALLIES NEVER LEAD
When a fighter is included in a warband as a hero or ally, if they have the **Leader** runemark (☀) on their fighter card, this runemark is only used to determine which abilities the fighter can use; the hero or ally is not considered to have the **Leader** runemark (☀) for any other purpose or rule. This means that any rule that refers to the leader of a warband does not refer to any heroes or allies in that warband.

MONSTERS AND THRALLS

The Eightpoints is home to more than just corrupted tribesmen. Monsters and beasts of all kinds dwell in this tainted land; the strongest warbands seek to bind such creatures to their will, though that is easier said than done…

MONSTERS

This section refers a type of fighter known as a **monster**. Monsters are fighters with the **Gargantuan** runemark (🔱).

If you have the *Warcry: Monsters and Mercenaries* expansion, the rules in this section supersede the monster rules in that book.

Monsters are subject to the following rules:

DEPLOYING MONSTERS

When monsters are deployed, they must be placed wholly within 5" horizontally of a deployment point instead of wholly within 3".

ACTIVATING MONSTERS

A monster can be activated 3 times in a battle round instead of only once, but each time it is activated, it can make only 1 action instead of 2. Each time a monster is activated, it can use 1 ability before or after its action.

If a monster makes a wait action, its activation immediately ends; the monster is not said to be waiting and the rules for waiting do not apply.

MOVE ACTIONS WITH MONSTERS

A monster can climb and jump like any other fighter; however, if at the end of a move action, its base is not wholly on a platform or the battlefield floor, it is said to have fallen.

If a monster is said to have fallen, any part of the model's base can be placed on the point picked by your opponent instead of just the centre.

MONSTER-HUNTING ABILITIES

If any monsters are in play, all fighters except the monsters themselves and fighters with the **Beast** runemark (🐗) can use the **Monster-hunting Abilities** shown opposite.

MONSTERS AND UNIVERSAL ABILITIES

Monsters cannot use universal abilities. Instead, if any monsters are in play, they can use the **Monster Abilities** shown opposite.

MONSTERS AND TREASURE

Monsters can never carry treasure.

THRALLS

On page 11, you will find fighter cards and abilities for 2 types of Thrall. Each of these fighters has the **Destruction** runemark (🗲) and the **Thrall** runemark (☿). These fighters can be included in Destruction warbands using the rules on page 49 of the Core Book.

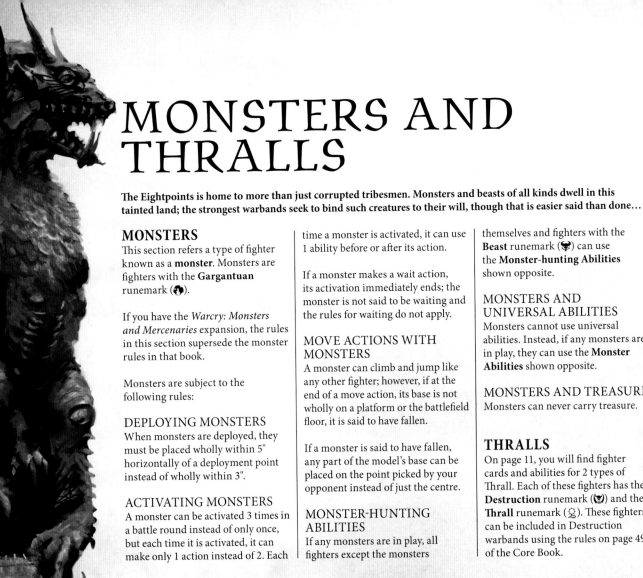

Troggoths are as dangerous as they are stupid, which means they are deadly indeed.

MONSTER-HUNTING ABILITIES

	[Double] Binding Ropes: Pick an enemy fighter with the **Gargantuan** runemark () within 1" of this fighter and roll a number of dice equal to the value of this ability. For each 4+, subtract 1 from the Move characteristic of that fighter (to a minimum of 3) until the end of the battle.
	[Double] Dodge and Evade: Until the end of the battle round, add the value of this ability to the Toughness characteristic of this fighter when it is being targeted by an attack action made by a fighter with the **Gargantuan** runemark ().
	[Double] Jump on its Back: Pick an enemy fighter with the **Gargantuan** runemark (). Until the end of the battle round, if that fighter starts a move action within 1" of this fighter, then after that move action, you can remove this fighter from the battlefield and set them up within 1" of that fighter.
	[Triple] Go for the Eyes: If the next attack action made by this fighter this activation that targets an enemy fighter with the **Gargantuan** runemark () scores any critical hits, subtract 1 from the Attacks characteristic (to a minimum of 1) of attack actions made by that fighter until the end of the battle.
	[Triple] Gutting Strike: Add the value of this ability to the damage points allocated by each critical hit from attack actions made by this fighter this activation that have a Range characteristic of 3 or less and that target an enemy fighter with the **Gargantuan** runemark ().
	[Quad] Taunt: Pick a visible enemy fighter with the **Gargantuan** runemark () that is within 6" of this fighter and roll a number of dice equal to the value of this ability. If a 4+ is rolled on any of the dice, then until the end of the battle round or until this fighter is taken down, attack actions made by that fighter must target this fighter.

MONSTER ABILITIES

	[Double] Monstrous Reach: Until the end of this fighter's activation, do not count the vertical distance when measuring the range for attack actions made by this fighter.
	[Triple] Drag and Maul: Pick a visible enemy fighter within 6" of this fighter. Remove that fighter from the battlefield and set them up within 1" of this fighter. Then, roll a number of dice equal to the value of this ability. For each 4+, allocate 3 damage points to that fighter.
	[Quad] Demolishing Rampage: Pick a terrain feature within 1" of this fighter. In an order of your choice, place each objective, treasure token and fighter that is on that terrain feature, and on any other terrain feature that is on that terrain feature, on the battlefield floor in a location of your choice as close as possible horizontally to its current location. Then, in an order of your choice, each fighter placed on the battlefield in this manner suffers impact damage. Then, remove the terrain feature(s).

USING MONSTERS IN YOUR BATTLES

Monsters can be used in games of Warcry in the following ways:

TWIST CARDS

Monsters with the **Chaotic Beasts** faction runemark (✹) can be used with any twist card that brings chaotic beasts into play.

INCLUDING MONSTERS IN YOUR WARBAND

Every monster in Warcry has one of the following faction runemarks:

- **Chaotic Beasts** (✹)
- **Monsters of Order** (🜊)
- **Monsters of Death** (🜋)
- **Monsters of Destruction** (🜍)

Destruction warbands can include monsters with the **Monsters of Destruction** faction runemark (🜍). You can find the monsters with this faction runemark on the following pages.

Additionally, the rules for including a monster in your warband vary depending on the style of game you are playing:

OPEN PLAY

In open play, when mustering for a battle, you can include 1 monster in your warband. Monsters cost points just like any other fighter but are ignored for the purposes of the rule that requires all fighters in a warband to share the same faction runemark.

NARRATIVE PLAY

In narrative play, winning certain challenge battles will allow you to add a monster to your warband roster. In this book, the challenge battles 'Gargantuan Carnage' (pg 59), 'The Big Carngrad Bash' (pg 60) and 'Picking Your Poison' (pg 62) allow a Destruction warband to do so. You can find the rules for challenge battles on pages 56-57.

Your warband roster can include no more than 1 monster at any time. If you have the option to add a new monster to your warband roster and you wish to do so, you must first remove the existing monster from your warband roster.

Like other fighters, monsters can receive destiny levels and players must make injury rolls for them. However, monsters can never bear lesser artefacts or artefacts of power and can never be chosen to become favoured warriors.

When mustering for a campaign battle, you can include 1 monster from your warband roster in your warband. Monsters cost points just like any other fighter but are ignored for the purposes of the rule that requires all fighters in a warband to share the same faction runemark.

In addition, if you are playing a convergence, only the Aspirant player can include any monsters in their warband.

MATCHED PLAY

Monsters cannot be included in warbands in matched play battles. However, if both players agree, players should feel free to use the open play rules for monsters in their matched play games to allow them to include 1 monster in their warband.

ALEGUZZLER GARGANT

Gargants are titanic, thuggish louts who traipse across the realms causing havoc wherever they go. On occasion, they may join forces with a warband of Destruction, often in return for a steady supply of meat, grog and violence.

DAMAGE TABLE

DAMAGE POINTS ALLOCATED	MOVE	DAMAGE
0-10	6	4/8
11-20	5	4/6
21-30	4	3/6
31-40	3	3/4
41-49	2	2/4

ALEGUZZLER GARGANT ABILITIES

[Double] Drunken Stagger: Roll a number of dice equal to the value of this ability. For each 1-2, subtract 1 from this fighter's Move characteristic until the end of this fighter's activation. For each 3+, add 1 to this fighter's Move characteristic until the end of this fighter's activation.

[Triple] Mighty Kick: Until the end of this fighter's activation, the next time this fighter finishes a move action within 1" of an enemy fighter, pick a visible enemy fighter within 1" of this fighter. Allocate a number of damage points to that fighter equal to the value of this ability.

[Quad] Vicious 'Eadbutt: Pick a visible enemy fighter within 1" of this fighter and roll a number of dice equal to the value of this ability. For each 4+, allocate a number of damage points to that fighter equal to the value of this ability.

SKITTERSTRAND ARACHNAROK

Bursting from their web-strewn lairs, Skitterstrand Arachnaroks strike without warning. Their monstrous fangs drip with deadly paralysing venom, and the fate of those dragged back to their nests is best left unconsidered.

DAMAGE TABLE

DAMAGE POINTS ALLOCATED	MOVE	DAMAGE
0-10	8	4/8
11-20	7	4/6
21-30	6	3/6
31-40	5	3/4
41-54	4	2/4

SKITTERSTRAND ARACHNAROK ABILITIES

[Double] Wall Crawler: Until the end of this fighter's activation, do not count the vertical distance moved when this fighter is climbing.

[Triple] Paralysing Venom: Until the end of this fighter's activation, after each attack action made by this fighter, roll a dice. On a 2+, until the end of the battle round, the target of that attack action cannot make move actions or disengage actions.

[Quad] Dragged Victim: Pick an enemy fighter within 1" of this fighter. Remove that fighter from the battlefield and set them up within 1" of this fighter. Then, this fighter makes a bonus attack action against that fighter.

DANKHOLD TROGGOTH

Troggoths are vile monsters born out of primordial, arcane gunge. Dankhold Troggoths are amongst the most dangerous of all troggoth sub-breeds, regenerating grievous wounds as easily as they crush their foes to paste.

DAMAGE TABLE

DAMAGE POINTS ALLOCATED	MOVE	DAMAGE
0-10	5	4/8
11-20	5	4/6
21-30	4	3/6
31-40	4	3/4
41-47	3	2/4

DANKHOLD TROGGOTH ABILITIES

 [Double] Squiggly-beast Followers: Roll a dice for each visible enemy fighter within 3" of this fighter. If the roll is less than or equal to the value of this ability, allocate 1 damage point to the fighter being rolled for.

 [Double] Troggoth Regrowth: Remove a number of damage points from this fighter equal to the value of this ability.

 [Triple] Crushing Grip: Pick 1 visible enemy fighter within 1" of this fighter and roll a number of dice equal to the value of this ability. For each 4+, allocate 2 damage points to that fighter.

The sight of a marauding Dankhold Troggoth is cause for wise warriors to flee.

DESTRUCTION THRALLS

When the mobs of Destruction trek across the Bloodwind Spoil, all manner of brutish beasts emerge from the caves to follow in their wake. Their strength, size and lack of hygiene sees them get on well with the warriors of Gorkamorka.

DESTRUCTION THRALL ABILITIES

	[Double] Noxious Vomit: Roll a number of dice equal to the value of this ability. For each 4+, pick 1 visible enemy fighter within 6" of this fighter. Allocate D3 damage points to that fighter.
	[Double] Troggoth Regrowth: Remove a number of damage points from this fighter equal to the value of this ability.

The stony skin of a Rockgut Troggoth can repel even the finest of blades.

WARBANDS OF DESTRUCTION

In this section, you will find all the rules needed to muster warbands of Destruction and use them in skirmish battles in the Bloodwind Spoil. Detailed background information explores the warlike, often bizarre cultures and motivations that drive these savage creatures to seek out new scraps, while a complete range of fighter cards details the profiles and points costs for all of the many warriors of Destruction available in Warcry.

In addition, the four warbands presented in this section also have access to unique ability tables, representing the brutal but kunnin' means by which they bludgeon their adversaries to a pulp and please their almighty twin-headed god.

'The trouble wiv humies is dat when you hit 'em, most of the time they don't get up again. Runty little gitz.'

GLOOMSPITE GITZ

The Gloomspite Gitz infest the dark and clammy places of the realms. These crazed troglodytes – be they grot or hungering cave-beast – are shroom-addled lunatics who delight in spreading their malice and spite.

To most mortals, the mean-spirited greenskins known as grots are little more than old washerwomen's tales. Cautionary rhymes and grisly fables about Grobi Blackcap, Boggart-the-Green, knocker-devyles and countless other impish creatures that lurk in the darkness are regularly employed to frighten Azyrite children into behaving. But grots are very real. Typically shorter than even a duardin, they possess beady red eyes, a long hooked nose, oversized ears and an absolute lack of anything approaching common decency. There are many types of grots found throughout the realms, but amongst the most dangerous are those subspecies who have taken to living in the dankest of environments. Along with the other inhabitants of their subterranean domains, these greenskins refer to themselves as the Gloomspite Gitz.

The average grot is not particularly courageous, intelligent, trustworthy or hygienic. They are opportunistic and impulsive creatures, prone to stabbing their mates in the back just for a laugh – so long as there's no chance of getting caught. Yet grots make up for these deficiencies in a variety of ways. They are remarkably cunning and exist in seemingly infinite numbers, no matter how many of them are slain. Their sense of self-preservation is strong, making them near impossible to root out once they have claimed a territory as their own.

The greatest strength of the grots, however, is their faith in the Bad Moon. Little is known of this ominous celestial entity; it appears in the skies of the realms seemingly at random, spreading madness and hideous fungal mutation in its wake. Most mortals are rightly terrified of the Bad Moon, for its coming is heralded by strange omens and leads to the disintegration all that is ordered. Nevertheless, the Gloomspite Gitz revere it as their god, for they believe it shall one day aid in bringing about the Everdank, a sacred time when all of creation will mirror the damp and mould-encrusted caverns in which they dwell. When bathed in the Bad Moon's clammy half-light, the grot hordes are filled with a frothing mania, boiling up to the surface in great tides to wreak wanton havoc.

The armies of the Gloomspite Gitz are madcap and disorderly, but they are no less deadly for it. The majority of their hordes are composed of the Moonclan skraps. Clad in thick black robes, these spiteful grots detest the sun – known to them as the mythical bogeyman Glareface Frazzlegit – and will only venture out under its punishing gaze in times of direst need. Led by shroom-crazed shamans, the bizarre wise-grots of the Gobbapalooza and the cunning warlords known as Loonbosses, they deploy all manner of unorthodox

yet terrifying warriors to 'teach the surface gitz a lesson', from packs of ravenous, bouncing fungus-beasts known as squigs to the deranged whirlwinds of death that are the Fanatics.

Yet other grot subcultures and cave creatures also march in the riotous armies of the Gloomspite Gitz. The venom-drinking Spiderfang Grots dwell in arboreal regions far from the sun's hateful glare, shrouded by thick webs and crooked trees that cluster in close. These grots are deranged even by the standards of their fellows. Over many centuries, they have learnt to tame – or at least appease – the gigantic spiders that infest their homes, in many cases even riding them into battle as a scuttering and highly mobile form of light cavalry. Whether through discovering sinister truths or simply being overwhelmed by the venomous bites of their arachnid familiars, the Webspinner Shamans who lead their stalktribes are said to receive visions from a monstrous deity known as the Spider God. At the shrieked decree of these spell-flingers, mobs of Spider Riders scuttle through the shadows across the realms, seeking out new toxic ingredients to empower the shamans' rituals.

Though the Eightpoints are one of the most inhospitable regions imaginable, the Gloomspite Gitz can still be found infesting the clammiest corners of Archaon's domain, clinging onto existence like a tenacious fungal infection. Their spore-choked lurklairs are secreted all across the Bloodwind Spoil, and no matter how many times they are raided by warriors seeking the Everchosen's favour, somehow the grots keep on turning up. It is even rumoured that they have managed to make ingress into the network of tunnels and warrens that run beneath Carngrad, though if this is true, the greenskins are smart enough to keep their heads down and not attract too much attention.

The Gloomspite Gitz of the Eightpoints know that they are in hostile territory, and thus their Sneaky Skraps only venture forth from their cavernous lairs when they believe they have good cause. Of course, what a grot considers to be good cause – which includes, but is not limited to, stealing bottles to fill with potent fungal brews, tracking down the boss's lost squig before he returns from a raid and being convinced to follow a particularly deranged shaman – would boggle the minds of most rational surface-dwellers. The grots don't give the strangeness of their deeds a second thought, however, and they relish any opportunity to vent their malicious cruelty on the isolated warbands that they encounter out amidst the wastes.

There is perhaps only one thing that could truly inspire the Gitz of the Eightpoints to rise en masse against the forces of Chaos: the Bad Moon itself waxing high over the lands of the Varanspire. Some Moonclan shamans and the warbands that accompany them have dedicated their existence to searching for mystical know-wotz and realmstone doo-dadz, determined to find some way to attract the lunar deity. Should they somehow succeed in their quest, then even the armies of the Everchosen may be hard-pressed by the resulting eruption of green-skinned anarchy.

15

GLOOMSPITE GITZ

What the Gloomspite Gitz lack in courage and skill, they make up for in numbers, cunning and spite. Wielding all manner of cruel pokin' weapons and accompanied by a veritable menagerie of troglodytic beasts, the green-skinned loons are a menace to all who encounter them.

GLOOMSPITE GITZ FIGHTER ABILITIES

[Double] Backstabbing Mob: A fighter can use this ability only if there is a visible friendly fighter within 1" of them. Until the end of this fighter's activation, add 1 to the Attacks and Strength characteristics of attack actions made by this fighter that have a Range characteristic of 3 or less.

[Double] Barbed Net: Pick a visible enemy fighter within 3" of this fighter and roll a dice. On a 3+, until the end of the battle round, that fighter cannot make move actions or disengage actions.

[Triple] Boing! Boing! Boing!: Until the end of this fighter's activation, the next time this fighter finishes a move action within 1" of an enemy fighter, pick a visible enemy fighter within 1" of this fighter. Allocate a number of damage points to that fighter equal to the value of this ability.

[Triple] Spider Bite: Pick a visible enemy fighter within 1" of this fighter and roll a number of dice equal to the value of this ability. For each 2-5, allocate 1 damage point to that fighter. For each 6, allocate 3 damage points to that fighter.

[Triple] Go Dat Way!: Pick a friendly fighter with the **Beast** runemark (🐾) within 4" of this fighter. That fighter makes a bonus move action.

[Quad] Sneaky Stab: This fighter makes a bonus move action. Then, they can make a bonus attack action. In addition, if the fighter targeted by that attack action is within 1" of this fighter, add the value of this ability to the damage points allocated by hits and critical hits from that attack action.

GLOOMSPITE GITZ LEADER ABILITIES

[Double] Speed of the Spider God: Until the end of the battle round, add 1 to the Move characteristic of friendly fighters with the **Destroyer** runemark (🏃) that are within 6" of this fighter when this fighter uses this ability.

[Triple] Stab 'Em Good: Until the end of the battle round, add 1 to the Attacks characteristic of attack actions that have a Range characteristic of 3 or less made by friendly fighters while they are within 6" of this fighter.

[Triple] Magic Spore Maws: Roll a dice for each visible enemy fighter within 3" of this fighter. On a 3-4, allocate 1 damage point to the fighter being rolled for. On a 5-6, allocate a number of damage points to the fighter being rolled for equal to the value of this ability.

[Quad] I'm Da Boss, Now Stab 'Em Good!: Until the end of the battle round, add the value of this ability to the Attacks characteristic of attack actions that have a Range characteristic of 3 or less made by friendly fighters while they are within 6" of this fighter.

GLOOMSPITE GITZ SNEAKY SKRAPS

LOONBOSS ON GIANT CAVE SQUIG
275

⚔	2	4	5	2/5

➵ 8 ☀ 5 💀 26

LOONBOSS
175

7	2	4	4	2/4

➵ 4 ☀ 4 💀 18

FUNGOID CAVE-SHAMAN
175

⚡	3-7	2	3	3/6
🏏	1	3	4	1/4

➵ 4 ☀ 3 💀 18

SCUTTLEBOSS
220

⚔	2	3	4	2/4

➵ 10 ☀ 4 💀 26

WEBSPINNER SHAMAN
150

⚡	3-7	2	3	3/6
🏏	1	3	3	1/4

➵ 4 ☀ 3 💀 16

SPIDER RIDER BOSS
220

🏹	3-12	3	3	1/3
⚔	2	3	3	2/4

➵ 10 ☀ 4 💀 22

MOONCLAN BOSS
150

🗡	1	4	4	2/4

➵ 4 ☀ 4 💀 16

SQUIG HOPPER BOSS
250

🗡	1	5	5	2/4

➵ 10 ☀ 4 💀 22

BOUNDER BOSS
265

⚔	2	4	5	2/5

➵ 8 ☀ 5 💀 24

SPIDER RIDER
150

⚔	🌙 3-12	✴ 2	✊ 3	🛡 1/3	☠
🗡	🌙 2	✴ 2	✊ 3	🛡 1/4	

➹ 10 ☀ 4 💀 16

SHOOTA
65

⚔	🌙 3-12	✴ 2	✊ 3	🛡 1/3
🗡	🌙 1	✴ 3	✊ 3	🛡 1/2

➹ 4 ☀ 3 💀 8

SNEAKY SNUFFLER
85

🦷	🌙 1	✴ 3	✊ 3	🛡 2/4

➹ 4 ☀ 3 💀 15

CAVE SQUIG
140

🦷	🌙 1	✴ 4	✊ 5	🛡 2/4	☠

➹ 4 ☀ 4 💀 15

STABBA WITH STABBA AND MOON SHIELD
70

🗡	🌙 1	✴ 3	✊ 3	🛡 1/3

➹ 4 ☀ 4 💀 8

SQUIG HERDER
45

🗡	🌙 1	✴ 3	✊ 3	🛡 1/2	↻

➹ 4 ☀ 3 💀 8

STABBA WITH POKIN' SPEAR AND MOON SHIELD
70

🗡	🌙 2	✴ 2	✊ 3	🛡 1/4

➹ 4 ☀ 4 💀 8

SQUIG HOPPER
200

🗡	🌙 1	✴ 4	✊ 5	🛡 2/4	✦
					⚑

➹ 10 ☀ 4 💀 16

STABBA WITH BARBED NET
45

🗡	🌙 1	✴ 3	✊ 3	🛡 1/2	☠

➹ 4 ☀ 3 💀 8

BOINGROT BOUNDER
220

🗡	🌙 2	✴ 3	✊ 5	🛡 2/5	✦
					⚑

➹ 8 ☀ 5 💀 18

GOBBAPALOOZA

The fighter cards on this page have both the **Gloomspite Gitz** faction runemark (☾) and the **Ally** runemark (◯). This means that each fighter can either be added to a Gloomspite Gitz warband as a normal fighter or included in another Destruction warband as an ally (pg 5).

GOBBAPALOOZA ABILITIES	
	[Double] Mesmerise: Pick an enemy fighter within a number of inches of this fighter equal to the value of this ability and roll a dice. On a 3+, until the end of the battle round, that fighter cannot make move actions or disengage actions.
	[Double] Loonshine Potion: Pick a visible friendly fighter within 3" of this fighter. Until the end of the battle round, add half the value of this ability (rounding up) to the Attacks characteristic of the next attack action made by that fighter that has a Range characteristic of 3 or less.
	[Double] Poison Brew: Pick a visible friendly fighter within 3" of this fighter. Until the end of the battle round, add the value of this ability to the Strength characteristic of the next attack action made by that fighter that has a Range characteristic of 3 or less.
	[Triple] Bogeyman Dance: Pick a visible friendly fighter within 6" of this fighter. Until the end of the battle round, add half the value of this ability (rounding up) to the Move characteristic of that fighter.
	[Triple] Fungoid Cloud: Pick an enemy fighter within a number of inches of this fighter equal to the value of this ability. Until the end of the battle round, subtract the value of this ability from the Attacks characteristic (to a minimum of 1) of attack actions made by that fighter.

BOGGLEYE — 85 — 2 | 3 | 3 | 1/4 — 4 | 3 | 12

SCAREMONGER — 85 — 1 | 4 | 3 | 1/4 — 4 | 3 | 16

SHROOMANCER — 85 — 2 | 3 | 3 | 1/4 — 4 | 3 | 12

BREWGIT — 85 — 1 | 4 | 3 | 1/3 — 4 | 3 | 12

SPIKER — 85 — 2 | 3 | 3 | 1/4 — 4 | 3 | 12

OGOR MAWTRIBES

Like a swarm of huge and hideous locusts, the ogors rampage across the realms in search of fresh meat. Each of these brutes is an insatiable glutton, trusting in a simple boast: 'First we're gonna beat it, then we're gonna eat it'.

The average ogor stands twice the height of a man and is considerably bulkier and more muscular to boot. Their limbs are thick and meaty, their bones as solid as the earth and their appetite truly legendary. The ogor way of life is centred entirely around gorging themselves; it is an all-consuming obsession and act of religious devotion, the means by which these creatures honour their god. If an ogor is not currently eating, they will almost certainly be thinking about doing so or fighting to secure their next meal. If the ogors had their way, they would devour the Mortal Realms in their entirety – and likely still be hungry for seconds.

The nomadic Mawtribes of the ogors are dominated by two very different cultures, united by their shared heritage and desire to crush and devour anything stupid enough to get in their way. The most common breed of ogors are known as the Gutbusters; their wandering warglutts can range from a single family of ogors to mighty hordes of many hundreds of the creatures. Guided by their holy gastromancers – the Butchers of Gorkamorka, the Gulping God – they have been a plague on civilised lands since the lost time of the Age of Myth. Fighting at the forefront of the great Mawpaths, they strip the lands bare of edible resources before returning to their Gluttholds, only to emerge once more when hunger compels them to do it all over again.

The Beastclaw Raider Alfrostuns, meanwhile, are mounted tribes that are burdened with a terrible curse. They must remain constantly on the move or risk being swallowed by the punishing cold of the mystical Everwinter that forever follows in their wake. These hardy ogors ride to battle upon fearsome predators and mighty ice-beasts, reducing the civilised kingdoms they ravage to frostbitten wastelands. The Beastclaw Raiders possess their own primitive but undeniably strong culture, complete with traditions, customs and even an ancestral language known as svoringar. Though the Beastclaw Alfrostuns often find themselves competing with the Gutbusters for pillaging rights, when a truly mighty ogor warlord comes to power, the hungering hordes unite – much to the misfortune of their enemies.

Most ogor warriors fall into the ranks of the Ogor Gluttons, taking simple satisfaction in battering their enemies to death with oversized clubs and cleavers. Veteran Ironguts serve as the personal thugs and drinking companions of a warglutt's Tyrant, while the cannon-totting Leadbelchers are obsessed with explosive destruction. Icebrow Hunters lead packs of Mournfang cavalry and the beasts of the winter wilds into battle, tracking foes

through the most inhospitable of terrain. Around them swarm diminutive gnoblars, malicious greenskins who love nothing more than kicking an enemy while they're down.

'Gobble the brains and gorge on the meat.

Chew on the eyes and crunch the feet.

Batter the softflesh and give 'em a prod,

Into the maw of the Gulping God.'

- One of many traditional ogor feasting songs

On occasion, representatives of more idiosyncratic ogor cultures may offer their services to a warband. Firebellies are flame-priests who worship Gorkamorka in the form of the Sun-eater. They travel far and wide in search of combustible materials, which they then devour in great bombastic rituals and use to belch forth sheets of scouring flame. Many Firebellies journey to the Eightpoints in search of these inflammable ingredients – or simply because they believe their volcano god told them to do so. These wandering shamans often join up with ogor warbands, where their volatile eccentricity is tolerated largely because of their magical prowess and ability to cook raw meat in a matter of moments.

Maneaters, meanwhile, are mercenaries who have fought, killed and devoured just about every kind of foe imaginable. Though they dress extravagantly and place a great deal of import on their hoarded wealth – largely because they like how it glitters – only a fool would underestimate the Maneaters. Their skills have been honed over a lifetime of battle, and they enjoy nothing more than proving their warlike prowess to 'little 'uns'.

The ogors do not come to the Eightpoints out of any great sense of duty or desire for power. These gluttonous brutes seek only two things from the lands of the Varanspire: new enemies to test themselves against and exotic foodstuffs to sample. Though the mutated and ruin-touched devotees of Chaos are something of an acquired taste to many ogors, there are nevertheless those warbands who seek out these exotic flavours above all others. The monsters that congregate in the Fangs mountain range and around the vast crimson lake known as Blood Lake Basin are favoured prey of the hungering Wanderglutts that stomp their way across the land. Those ogors who travel to these hunting grounds regularly find themselves drawn into battle against roving packs of the Untamed Beasts and mobs of savage Bonesplitterz for the glory of chasing down the most hideous creatures and messily consuming their tough, vital flesh.

Though most ogors can be described as being as thick as two planks, it is also true that they have enough sense to know how to nail these planks together and bludgeon their enemies with them. As such, they are the only race of Destruction to truly grasp the value of mercenary work. While orruks may baulk at the idea of not fighting everyone they come across, ogors know full well that the softflesh – that is, anyone smaller than they are – can often be persuaded to offer regular tribute of food and shiny stuff in return for having their enemies stomped flat. It doesn't matter one bit to the ogors that such arrangements typically end poorly for their paymasters – after all, today's ally is simply tomorrow's appetiser.

OGOR MAWTRIBES

A warband of ogors is a gathering of ravenous bullies who take a brutish delight in exerting their strength over anything punier than they are. Each of these gluttonous monsters is incredibly hard to kill, and with a single punch, they can crush skulls or dent even the heaviest armour.

OGOR MAWTRIBES FIGHTER ABILITIES

[Double] On the Mawpath: Add half the value of this ability (rounding up) to the Move characteristic of this fighter for the next move action they make this activation.

[Double] Bounding Leaps: A fighter can use this ability only if there is a visible enemy fighter within 6" of them. This fighter makes a bonus move action and must finish closer to the closest visible enemy fighter than they were at the start of that move action.

[Double] Ironfist: Pick a visible enemy fighter within 1" of this fighter and roll 2 dice. For each 4-5, allocate 1 damage point to that fighter. For each 6, allocate a number of damage points to that fighter equal to the value of this ability.

[Triple] Bullcharge: Until the end of this fighter's activation, the next time this fighter finishes a move action within 1" of an enemy fighter, pick a visible enemy fighter within 1" of this fighter. Allocate a number of damage points to that fighter equal to the value of this ability.

[Triple] Sneaky Traps: Until the end of the battle round, each time an enemy fighter finishes a move action within 3" of this fighter, that fighter suffers impact damage.

[Quad] Thunderous Blast of Hot Metal: Add half the value of this ability (rounding up) to the Attacks and Strength characteristics of the next attack action made by this fighter this activation that targets an enemy fighter more than 3" away.

OGOR MAWTRIBES LEADER ABILITIES

[Double] Might Makes Right: A fighter can use this ability only if an enemy fighter has been taken down by an attack action made by them this activation. This fighter makes a bonus move action or a bonus attack action.

[Double] Lead the Skal: Pick a visible friendly fighter with the **Beast** runemark (🐾) within 4" of this fighter. That friendly fighter makes a bonus attack action.

[Double] Bloodgruel: Add half the value of this ability (rounding up) to the Strength characteristic of the next attack action made by this fighter this activation that has a Range characteristic of 3 or more.

[Triple] Bully of the First Degree: Pick another friendly fighter that is visible and within 2" of this fighter. Allocate a number of damage points to that friendly fighter equal to half the value of this ability (rounding up). Then, that friendly fighter makes a bonus move action or a bonus attack action.

[Quad] Fire Breath: Allocate a number of damage points equal to the value of this ability to all visible enemy fighters within 3" of this fighter.

OGOR MAWTRIBES WANDERGLUTTS

MOURNFANG PACK WITH CULLING CLUB AND IRONFIST — 240

⚔	↩	✦	✊	🛡
1	3	5	3/6

➤ 8 | ☀ 4 | 💀 35

OGOR GLUTTON WITH CLUBS — 205

⚔	↩	✦	✊	🛡
1	4	5	3/6

➤ 4 | ☀ 4 | 💀 30

MOURNFANG PACK WITH GARGANT HACKER — 245

⚔	↩	✦	✊	🛡
1	2	5	4/8

➤ 8 | ☀ 4 | 💀 35

OGOR GLUTTON WITH IRONFIST — 200

⚔	↩	✦	✊	🛡
1	3	5	3/6

➤ 4 | ☀ 4 | 💀 30

MANEATER — 220

⚔	↩	✦	✊	🛡
8	2	3	1/4
1	3	5	3/6

➤ 4 | ☀ 4 | 💀 30

IRONGUT — 235

⚔	↩	✦	✊	🛡
1	2	6	4/8

➤ 4 | ☀ 5 | 💀 30

FROST SABRE — 170

⚔	↩	✦	✊	🛡
1	4	4	2/5

➤ 8 | ☀ 4 | 💀 20

LEADBELCHER — 230

⚔	↩	✦	✊	🛡
3-10	3	5	3/6
1	3	4	1/4

➤ 4 | ☀ 4 | 💀 30

ICEFALL YHETEE — 185

⚔	↩	✦	✊	🛡
1	4	4	2/5

➤ 8 | ☀ 4 | 💀 25

GNOBLAR — 45

⚔	↩	✦	✊	🛡
1	3	3	1/3

➤ 4 | ☀ 3 | 💀 8

GORGER — 175

⚔	↩	✦	✊	🛡
1	4	4	3/6

➤ 5 | ☀ 3 | 💀 30

The tough, weathered flesh of the Untamed Beasts is not considered the finest of ogor delicacies, but to deny themselves the feast would be to blaspheme against the Gulping God.

ORRUK WARCLANS

Brutish and bellicose, the orruk race lives only for war. These green-skinned marauders have fought all across the Mortal Realms and are never happier than when in the midst of utter carnage.

The booming war cry of the orruks signals the doom of empires. These thuggish creatures exist solely to fight; if an orruk is not already in the midst of a raging brawl, it is only because he is looking for a better scrap elsewhere. They are hulking, muscular creatures with tusked bucket jaws, leathery green flesh and porcine red eyes glaring from beneath heavyset brows. Though orruks are not intelligent per se, only a fool would underestimate them. They can be surprisingly innovative when called upon, especially in devising ways to smash their enemies, and the bloody-minded determination that characterises their psychology renders them almost unstoppable once set to a task. If an orruk decides to do something, he will give it his belligerent all – albeit with plenty of mindless violence along the way.

Orruks are the children of Gorkamorka, the two-headed god of primal destruction. In the Age of Myth, they fought alongside Sigmar's pantheon, for they acknowledged the 'Hammer God' as a worthy patron of warriors – the only being to ever bring Gorkamorka to a stalemate in a fair fight. For a time, they were content in their role as hunters, cleansing the realms of the predators that haunted the wastelands. But those days are long gone. Now the orruks fight purely for the joy of it and, though they may not realise it, to keep the wild lands pure from what they see as the undermining influence of civilisation.

Orruks despise false strength; they consider anything that grants artificial might – from the sturdy walls and innovative technologies of mankind's cities to the dark rituals of resurrection that fuel Nagash's necrotopia – to be deserving only of utter annihilation. To them, might makes right: the strong should prosper, and the weak should perish.

This barbarous philosophy has often earned them disdain from the loremasters of Sigmar's empire, but the ramshackle green-skinned armies care nothing for such haughty judgement. After all, no amount of knowledge will protect those soft-skinned know-it-alls from the business end of a choppa.

'Green iz best. Now, some of da Chaos boyz is green, but dey're slow and smell pretty funny to boot. We'll show 'em who da real green god is when we stomp their 'eads in. Waaagh!'

- Brute Boss Tranka da Big

Orruk society, such as it is, can be divided into warclans, each of which has its own culture and 'taktikz'. At the heart of the Waaagh! – a term for the great green crusades of violence that sweep the realms (and

26

that also doubles as an ear-splitting battle cry) – stomp the Ironjawz. These rampaging orruks epitomise the most brutal side of their race's psyche, and they are obsessed with demonstrating their might through displays of wanton violence. They wear the heaviest armour and wield the most impressive weapons, all the better to prove how tough they are. The Ironjawz are despoilers and destroyers, and were they to have their way, the realms would be reduced to barren wastelands in which the creed of the orruks would reign supreme. Armoured Brutes, eager Ardboys and mounted Gore-gruntas mass around the mightiest bosses. Gibbering spell-flingers and raging Warchanters channel the power of the Waaagh!, driving the boyz onwards to crash into the terrified foe.

Charging alongside the Ironjawz come the crazed Bonesplitterz. No orruk is born a Bonesplitter; rather, those greenskins who are driven mad by Waaagh! energy raging endlessly around their skulls will leave their former warclans behind and seek out gatherings of their feral kin. Clad in little more than mystic warpaint and led by war-dancing shamans, the Bonesplitterz are on a mission to hunt and slay the greatest monsters they can find. They do this not only because it offers a worthy fight but also because they believe that by slaughtering these beasts, they free the spirit of Gorkamorka trapped within their bones – and inherit some of his power in the process. Wielding bone weapons, oversized spears and their own raw muscle, the Bonesplitterz attack in a storm of blows that can easily overwhelm even the sturdiest of enemies.

The orruks are one of the most erratic races to have ended up in the Bloodwind Spoil. There is simply no way to tell when a raging mob of greenskins will suddenly surge forth from the wilds; several outer districts of Carngrad have been rocked more than once by these small-scale Waaagh!s – though the orruks are sufficiently kunnin' to leave enough standing to be rebuilt and thus smashed up again later. The majority of orruk warbands arrive in the Eightpoints after chasing an enemy through a 'funny-lookin'' portal or otherwise form when lost greenskins eventually wander into one another. They are ruthlessly hunted by the Chaos tribes, which suits the orruks just fine, for it means that a proper scrap is never far away.

Many Ironjawz warbands, sometimes known as Krushamobz for their vandalising tendencies, have begun targeting monoliths raised by the warlords of the Bloodwind Spoil, knocking over and defacing these structures with brutish glee in order to attract the attention of the toughest enemies. The Rangin' Rukks of the Bonesplitterz, meanwhile, have decided on a holy mission of their own: they believe the Varanspire itself to be the mightiest predator of the wastes, and with the rising of each bloody dawn, they make their way closer to its cyclopean magnificence, determined to slay it and absorb its power.

BONESPLITTERZ

Nobody can ever quite predict what the Bonesplitterz will do in a fight, least of all the orruks themselves. Clad in mystical warpaint and wielding crude but effective weapons, these crazed maniaks charge forward with a boundless energy, howling and gibbering as they run down the hapless foe.

BONESPLITTERZ FIGHTER ABILITIES

	[Double] Charge!: A fighter can use this ability only if there is a visible enemy fighter within 6" of them. This fighter makes a bonus move action and must finish closer to the closest visible enemy fighter than they were at the start of that move action.
	[Double] Toof Shiv: Pick a visible enemy fighter within 1" of this fighter and roll a dice. On a 3-4, allocate 1 damage point to that fighter. On a 5-6, allocate a number of damage points to that fighter equal to the value of this ability.
	[Double] Beast Spirit Ju-ju: Until the end of the battle round, add 1 to the Toughness characteristic of friendly fighters while they are within 6" of this fighter.
	[Triple] Tusker Charge: Until the end of this fighter's activation, the next time this fighter finishes a move action within 1" of an enemy fighter, pick a visible enemy fighter within 1" of this fighter. Allocate a number of damage points to that fighter equal to the value of this ability.
	[Triple] Loadsa Arrows: Add half the value of this ability (rounding up) to the Attacks characteristic of the next attack action made by this fighter this activation that targets an enemy fighter more than 3" away.
	[Quad] Rampaging Destroyer: Until the end of this fighter's activation, add 1 to the Attacks characteristic of attack actions made by this fighter. In addition, each time an enemy fighter is taken down by an attack action made by this fighter this activation, this fighter can make a bonus move action.

BONESPLITTERZ LEADER ABILITIES

	[Double] Weird Squig: Add 1 to the Attacks characteristic of attack actions made by this fighter this activation that target an enemy fighter more than 3" away.
	[Triple] Waaagh!: Add the value of this ability to the Move characteristic of friendly fighters within 6" of this fighter when this fighter uses this ability, until the end of the battle round.
	[Triple] Ritual Dance: Remove 1 damage point allocated to each friendly fighter within 6" of this fighter.
	[Triple] Beast-mask Dance: Until the end of the battle round, subtract 1 from the Attacks characteristic (to a minimum of 1) of attack actions made by enemy fighters while they are within 6" of this fighter.
	[Quad] Mighty Waaagh!: Add the value of this ability to the Move characteristic of friendly fighters within 9" of this fighter when this fighter uses this ability, until the end of the battle round.

BONESPLITTERZ RANGIN' RUKKS

SAVAGE BIG BOSS — 225

	1	3	5	3/6	

4 | 4 | 30

SAVAGE ORRUK BOSS WITH CHOMPA AND BONE SHIELD — 185

	1	4	4	2/5	

4 | 4 | 25

WURRGOG PROPHET — 225

	3-7	2	3	3/6	
	2	3	4	1/4	

4 | 4 | 28

SAVAGE ORRUK MORBOY BOSS — 205

	1	4	4	3/6	

4 | 4 | 25

WARDOKK — 205

	3-7	2	3	3/6	
	1	3	3	1/3	

4 | 4 | 25

SAVAGE ARROW BOSS — 125

	3-15	3	3	1/3	
	1	3	3	2/4	

4 | 4 | 25

MANIAK WEIRDNOB — 285

	3-7	2	3	3/6	
	2	3	4	1/4	

10 | 4 | 35

SAVAGE BOARBOY BOSS — 250

	1	4	4	2/5	

10 | 4 | 35

SAVAGE BOSS MANIAK — 265

	1	4	4	3/6	

10 | 4 | 35

SAVAGE BOARBOY WITH CHOMPA

150

1	3	3	1/3

10 | 4 | 25

SAVAGE BOARBOY WITH SAVAGE STIKKA

145

2	2	3	1/3

10 | 4 | 25

SAVAGE BOARBOY BONE TOTEM BEARER

205

3	3	5	2/4

10 | 4 | 25

SAVAGE BOARBOY MANIAK

170

1	3	4	2/4

10 | 3 | 25

SAVAGE ORRUK WITH SAVAGE STIKKA AND BONE SHIELD

85

2	2	3	1/3

4 | 4 | 15

SAVAGE ORRUK WITH CHOMPA AND BONE SHIELD

90

1	3	3	1/3

4 | 4 | 15

SAVAGE BIG STABBAS

175

1	3	5	3/6

4 | 3 | 30

SAVAGE ORRUK MORBOY

110

1	3	4	2/4

4 | 3 | 15

SAVAGE ORRUK MORBOY BONE TOTEM BEARER

110

3	3	4	2/4

4 | 3 | 15

SAVAGE ORRUK ARROWBOY

90

3-15	2	3	1/3
1	3	3	1/2

4 | 3 | 15

The ravings of a Wurrgog Prophet might seem unintelligible to most, but to the Bonesplitterz they are holy commands that must be obeyed.

IRONJAWZ

There is nothing subtle about the Ironjawz way of war. Clad in the heaviest pig-iron plates and wielding huge cleavers and smashas, these hulking orruks stomp forward under the command of their bellowing bosses, eager to close with the enemy and crush them into a fine and gory paste.

IRONJAWZ FIGHTER ABILITIES

[Double] Charge!: A fighter can use this ability only if there is a visible enemy fighter within 6" of them. This fighter makes a bonus move action and must finish closer to the closest visible enemy fighter than they were at the start of that move action.

[Double] Shield Bash: After this fighter's next move action this activation, pick a visible enemy fighter within 1" of this fighter and roll a dice. On a 4-5, allocate 1 damage point to that fighter. On a 6, allocate a number of damage points to that fighter equal to the value of this ability.

[Double] Duff Up Da Big Thing: Until the end of this fighter's activation, add 2 to the Attacks and Strength characteristics of attack actions made by this fighter that have a Range characteristic of 3 or less and that target an enemy fighter with a Wounds characteristic of 15 or more.

[Triple] Gore-grunta Charge: Until the end of this fighter's activation, the next time this fighter finishes a move action within 1" of an enemy fighter, pick a visible enemy fighter within 1" of this fighter. Allocate a number of damage points to that fighter equal to the value of this ability.

[Quad] Rampaging Destroyer: Until the end of this fighter's activation, add 1 to the Attacks characteristic of attack actions made by this fighter. In addition, each time an enemy fighter is taken down by an attack action made by this fighter this activation, this fighter can make a bonus move action.

IRONJAWZ LEADER ABILITIES

[Double] Warchanter's Beat: Until the end of the battle round, add 1 to the Attacks characteristic of attack actions that have a Range characteristic of 3 or less made by friendly fighters while they are within 6" of this fighter.

[Triple] Foot of Gork: Pick a visible enemy fighter within 12" of this fighter and roll a number of dice equal to the value of this ability. For each 2-5, allocate 1 damage point to that fighter. For each 6, allocate 3 damage points to that fighter.

[Triple] Waaagh!: Add the value of this ability to the Move characteristic of friendly fighters within 6" of this fighter when this fighter uses this ability, until the end of the battle round.

[Triple] Da Grab an' Bash: Pick a visible enemy fighter within 1" of this fighter and roll a dice. On a 3+, until the end of the battle round, that fighter cannot make move actions or disengage actions. In addition, on a 6, this fighter can make a bonus attack action against that enemy fighter.

[Quad] Mighty Waaagh!: Add the value of this ability to the Move characteristic of friendly fighters within 9" of this fighter when this fighter uses this ability, until the end of the battle round.

IRONJAWZ KRUSHAMOBZ

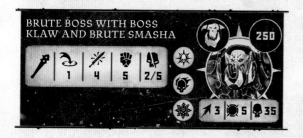

ORRUK GORE-GRUNTA WITH JAGGED GORE-HACKA
210

	2	2	5	2/4

8 | 4 | 35

ORRUK BRUTE WITH GORE-CHOPPA
200

	1	3	5	3/6

3 | 5 | 25

ORRUK GORE-GRUNTA WITH PIG-IRON CHOPPA
205

	1	3	4	2/4

8 | 4 | 35

ORRUK ARDBOY WITH ARDBOY CHOPPAS
110

	1	4	4	1/4

3 | 4 | 15

ORRUK BRUTE WITH PAIR OF BRUTE CHOPPAS
180

	1	4	4	2/4

3 | 5 | 25

ORRUK ARDBOY WITH ARDBOY CHOPPA AND ORRUK-FORGED SHIELD
125

	1	3	4	1/4

3 | 5 | 15

ORRUK BRUTE WITH JAGGED GORE-HACKA
180

	1	3	5	2/4

3 | 5 | 25

ORRUK ARDBOY WITH ARDBOY BIG CHOPPA
110

	1	3	4	2/4

3 | 4 | 15

Ironjawz prefer a stand-up fight where possible, but they won't say no to battling sneakier foes – provided they still get to snap some limbs.

BACKGROUND TABLES

The forces of Destruction are some of the most entertaining factions to command in Warcry narrative play. These boisterous and belligerent mobs bring with them the ability to wreak utter havoc as well as a sense of humour and fun that appeals to a great many gamers. The adventures – or perhaps misadventures – that your lads will embark upon are sure to stick in your mind long after the final dice have been rolled, and many players enjoy naming and personalising their fighters to add their own stamp to these brutish louts.

On the following pages, you will find a series of naming tables for various Destruction warbands, together with background generators that allow you to add personality to your leader and warband as a whole. Whether you use these 'off the page' or simply take them as inspiration, they'll be sure to add a fun new narrative element to your games.

'Dey call me Krizza da Kreep. Dat is, when I ain't already kreeped up behind the zoggers and shivved 'em good and proppa.'

BONESPLITTERZ

Even other orruks regard Bonesplitterz with a certain degree of caution, for these savage greenskins have fully embraced the feral spirit of Gorkamorka.

It is the visions of the Wurrgog Prophets that guide the Bonesplitterz to war. These thoroughly deranged shamans interpret portents and signs from the Great Green God. They then direct their tribe to battle, channelling the immense power of Waaagh! energy to drive the Bonesplitterz into a frenzy of destruction. Not all of Gorkamorka's commands are so straightforward, however. The Bonesplitterz are utterly unpredictable, and attempting to divine their intentions is a fool's game. It is not unheard of for a Wurrgog Prophet to send several of his warriors rampaging across the realms in pursuit of some strange and distant goal.

BONESPLITTERZ FIRST NAMES	
D10	**NAME**
1	Grozgak
2	Korgakk
3	Badbrukk
4	Krakkzog
5	Kragg
6	Worgutz
7	Orgakk
8	Rogga
9	Murgg
10	Ugdrak

BONESPLITTERZ LAST NAMES	
D10	**NAME**
1	Rokkskull
2	Gutklaw
3	Wildtompa
4	Snagtoof
5	Weirdskull
6	Snakechompa
7	Stonejawz
8	Krookfang
9	Eadkrakka
10	Madskull

ORIGIN	
1	**Howling Mad** – Your warband consists of the tribe's most battle-crazed lunatics.
2	**Glory Hunters** – Your warriors seek to prove themselves by committing the most reckless acts of violence.
3	**Heralds of the Waaagh!** – Your warriors believe that where they roam, the power of the Waaagh! swells.
4	**Painted Ones** – Your warriors have been marked with sacred runes by their tribe's Wurrgog Prophet.
5	**Lost** – You took a wrong turn somewhere, but your warriors are happy enough with where they ended up.
6	**Bone Hunters** – Your warband relentlessly hunts the largest predators, hoping to take their bones.

LEADER/FAVOURED WARRIOR BACKGROUND	
1	**Unpredictable Maniak** – Attempting to predict this warrior's actions is utterly pointless.
2	**Old Rival** – This warrior keeps the mouldering head of a hated rival, which they often argue with.
3	**Relentless** – This warrior never pauses for a moment; they simply barrel relentlessly forwards.
4	**Head Wound** – Having taken a nasty blow to the head, this warrior babbles a stream of nonsense.
5	**Great Hunter** – This warrior has hunted and killed some of the most ferocious beasts of Ghur.
6	**Unaccountably Lucky** – This warrior is blessed by Gorkamorka, somehow surviving every disaster.

GLOOMSPITE GITZ

Cruel, cunning and treacherous, the Gloomspite Gitz infest the dank places of the Mortal Realms like a mouldering fungus. Though anarchic creatures by their very nature, when they unite under a common cause, they are capable of wholescale destruction.

There are few regions of the realms untroubled by grots. Despite their diminutive size and natural cowardice, these greenskins are remarkably adaptable, somehow managing to thrive in the most hostile conditions. Those scattered tribes that dwell within the Eightpoints are particularly resilient. Chaos warlords irritated by the creatures' scavenging and pillaging often launch purges in an attempt to wipe them out, but should even a few grots manage to flee from the slaughter, their numbers soon begin to swell once more.

GLOOMSPITE GITZ FIRST NAMES	
D10	Name
1	Skitrag
2	Gripe
3	Snikka
4	Zotbag
5	Norg
6	Shiv
7	Flug
8	Kribba
9	Grark
10	Gitgrik

GLOOMSPITE GITZ LAST NAMES	
D10	Name
1	Neckstabba
2	Eyepoka
3	Pincha
4	Curdletongue
5	Nosebita
6	Skuttlestab
7	Toerag
8	Longears
9	Mooneye
10	Sourtongue

	ORIGIN
1	**Bottle Thieves** – Your warband specialises in pilfering glasswork from the bigger races.
2	**Shroomheads** – Your warband seeks out particularly noxious clusters of mushrooms to sample.
3	**Loon's Luck** – Your warband has survived many disasters, and your warriors believe themselves invulnerable.
4	**Exiles** – Your warriors have been judged unbearable even by their fellow grots, and your warband has been exiled into the wilds.
5	**Sneaky Backstabbers** – Your warriors are particularly good at moving about unseen.
6	**Eyepokers** – Your warriors are experts at the old grot tactic of aiming for the foe's most vulnerable areas.

	LEADER/FAVOURED WARRIOR BACKGROUND
1	**Babbling Loon** – Too many looncap mushrooms have robbed this warrior of the ability to speak coherently.
2	**Touched by the Clammy Hand** – This warrior is convinced that they are destined for great things.
3	**Wicked Tongue** – This warrior enjoys taunting their foes with jibes and unpleasant songs.
4	**Cowardly Git** – This warrior will only risk taking on their opponents when they are fully distracted.
5	**Foul Temper** – This warrior is particularly venomous and cruel, even for a grot.
6	**Strange Growth** – A bizarre fungal growth plagues this warrior, who insists it is a gift from the Bad Moon.

IRONJAWZ

The Ironjawz are the biggest and hardest orruks of all. Clad in pig-iron armour and swinging enormous, bone-breaking weapons, they wreak untold devastation across the realms.

It is rare to see a small group of orruks alone in enemy lands, for these creatures more usually gather into vast, rampaging hordes. Such bands are typically the remnant of a far larger host that has, by some miracle, been defeated. Still driven by a boisterous and uncontrollable love of violence, these orruk warbands look to cause as much destruction as possible, seeking out foes to battle and enemy outposts to crush into rubble. Despite their small numbers, these warbands can wreak a huge amount of damage. Several have been spotted amidst the wilds of the Eightpoints and thus far have crushed all those sent to slay them.

IRONJAWZ FIRST NAMES	
D10	**Name**
1	Drakka
2	Grukk
3	Skrug
4	Urgok
5	Rezgut
6	Grokk
7	Tranka
8	Drog
9	Zagga
10	Krakkfist

IRONJAWZ LAST NAMES	
D10	**Name**
1	Deffskull
2	Headstompa
3	Nekksnappa
4	Bigtoof
5	Rokknut
6	Fireklaw
7	Blakfist
8	da Biggest
9	Bonekruncha
10	Meaneye

	ORIGIN
1	**Siege Smashers** – Your warriors delight in smashing their way through fortifications and defences.
2	**Da Megaboss's Boyz** – Your warband once fought at the side of an Ironjawz Megaboss.
3	**Grotkickers** – Your warriors delight in bullying and brutalising those weaker than them.
4	**Only the 'Ardest** – Your warriors are the toughest and meanest survivors of a shattered Ironjawz brawl.
5	**Uneasy Alliance** – Each of your warriors are vying for command, through methods both brutal and kunnin'.
6	**Filled with Waaagh!** – Your warriors resonate with furious Waaagh! energy.

	LEADER/FAVOURED WARRIOR BACKGROUND
1	**Shiny Trophy** – This warrior's prized possession was stripped from the corpse of a defeated foe.
2	**Unstoppable** – This warrior just keeps going, even when stricken by grievous wounds.
3	**Boisterous Laughter** – This warrior loves the crash of combat so much that they boom with laughter when in battle.
4	**Brutal but Kunnin'** – Despite their innate savagery, this warrior can be surprisingly devious.
5	**Berserk Lunatic** – This warrior does not stop hacking at their foes until they are piles of splattered meat.
6	**Stubborn Brute** – When this warrior encounters a problem, they simply batter their way through it.

OGOR MAWTRIBES

Towering monsters even bulkier than an Ironjaw Brute, ogors are a plague on the Mortal Realms. Their wandering Mawtribes are akin to a swarm of hulking locusts, voraciously devouring all before them.

Ogors can always be described as either eating or hungry. Worshipping Gorkamorka in his aspect as the Gulping God, they are on a mission to consume everything they can. From the ravening Gutbusters to the winter-touched Beastclaw Raiders, all ogors are united by their desire to gorge themselves. The only thing an ogor enjoys almost as much as eating is a good fight, and the Eightpoints provide opportunity for both of these things in abundance. More and more warbands of ogors have been making their way to this interstitial realm, to the misfortune of everyone who crosses their path.

D10	OGOR MAWTRIBES FIRST NAMES
1	Balrak
2	Horg
3	Garl
4	Growt
5	Marg
6	Tulok
7	Asger
8	Tarfgar
9	Braggoth
10	Hrothgur

D10	OGOR MAWTRIBES LAST NAMES
1	Marrowbreath
2	Bloodgulper
3	Blacktooth
4	Gutgobbler
5	the Crusher
6	Harkorg
7	Iceblood
8	Beastcruncher
9	Bjarkarl
10	Vardok

	ORIGIN
1	**Wandering Mercenaries** – In return for bountiful supplies of food, your warriors will fight for just about anyone.
2	**Path of Destruction** – The winding Mawpath followed by your tribe has led you and your warriors to the Eightpoints.
3	**Exotic Palate** – Your warriors are forever seeking new and innovative tastes to sample.
4	**Exiled** – Your warriors were banished from the Mawtribe and now seek to forge their own destiny.
5	**Brothers in Bludgeoning** – You and your warriors are all part of the same family unit.
6	**Ahead of the Blizzard** – Your warband strives to outpace the furious Everwinter, going so far as to seek refuge in the lands of the Varanspire.

	LEADER/FAVOURED WARRIOR BACKGROUND
1	**Touched by the Gulping God** – This warrior once ate some particularly spoiled meat and now receives strange visions from their hungering deity.
2	**All Muscle** – Even amongst their hulking kind, this warrior's strength is legendary.
3	**Been There, Done That** – There are few foes this warrior has not fought and devoured at some point.
4	**Kineater** – This warrior once consumed their own siblings to prove their might.
5	**Ravenous Cravings** – This warrior has an insatiable desire for a particular foodstuff.
6	**Harbinger of Winter** – The icy chill of the Everwinter permanently clings to this warrior.

CAMPAIGNS AND CHALLENGES

In the following section, you will find four new fated quests available to Destruction warbands. These madcap escapades will take you far and wide across the Bloodwind Spoil. From the back alleys of Carngrad to the slave camps of Chaos warlords, you'll smash, bash and fight your way through all manner of foes, overcoming tough convergences to emerge triumphant. Like all fated quests, the ending of these tales is up to you to decide: will you take the honourable – and often brutal – path, or will you exercise your kunnin' for a chance at glory?

For those looking to prove themselves to be the mightiest of all bosses, six challenge battles will see your warband tackle bespoke scenarios in pursuit of greatness. The prizes for completing these are well worth it, among them the chance to unleash some truly titanic beasts of war!

'Either move aside or be smashed aside, softflesh. Don't much matter to me.'

DESTRUCTION FATED QUESTS

Warriors fight for many reasons, be it the pursuit of treasure, lust for power or a simple love of war. Those who battle amidst the Bloodwind Spoil are no different, though each warlord's story is defined by their choices and character.

In this section, you will find 4 special campaign quests known as **fated quests**. To use these quests, refer to page 63 of the Core Book.

HARBINGERS OF DESTRUCTION

The fated quests in this book each have the **Destruction** runemark (🗲). This means they can only be embarked upon by Destruction warbands.

When embarking upon one of these fated quests, you can choose 1 Destruction faction runemark to apply to the fated quest (pg 4).

The fated quests in this book use the territory rules opposite.

DESTRUCTION FATED QUEST TERRITORY RULES

Dominate Territory: *As the power of a warband grows, so too does the extent of the territory to which it can lay claim.*

You can spend 10 glory points to dominate a territory. Mark on your warband roster how many territories you dominate.

Dominating territory offers the following bonus:

For each territory dominated by your warband, increase the points you have available to spend on fighters when mustering your warband for a campaign battle by 50.

In addition, for each territory dominated by your warband, you can include 1 thrall in your warband when mustering for a campaign battle.

Thralls included in this manner are not added to your warband roster and cost points like any other fighter. Thralls can never gain destiny levels, bear artefacts or be chosen to become a favoured warrior.

TERRAIN CARDS

The terrain cards for the fated quests in this book use scenery models from *Warcry: Catacombs*.

If you do not have the scenery models from *Warcry: Catacombs* but you do have scenery models from either a Ravaged Lands terrain set or the older *Warcry Starter Set*, the player controlling the Adversary warband can choose one of the terrain cards from that set to use instead.

HONOUR OR GLORY

Even the most noble champion may occasionally sully their soul in pursuit of glory, while a black-hearted rogue might reveal themselves to possess a shred of honour – albeit only if it benefits them to show it. In the corrupted lands of the Eightpoints, it is a warrior's deeds alone that define them and chart the course of their destiny.

The campaign outcomes for fated quests differ from those in the Core Book. When you complete a fated quest, you have to make a choice between **Honour** or **Glory** before you claim your reward.

If you choose Glory, your reward will be an artefact of power.

If you choose Honour, your reward will be an **exalted** command trait.

EXALTED COMMAND TRAITS

Exalted command traits represent qualities so strong that they come to define a warrior for the rest of their life.

The first time you receive an exalted command trait, it must be given to your leader, and it replaces any existing command trait that they might have.

Once your leader has been given an exalted command trait, any future exalted command traits received are discarded.

Exalted command traits can never be given to a favoured warrior.

A LONG NIGHT IN CARNGRAD

FIRST CONVERGENCE
Run-down Tavern

SECOND CONVERGENCE
Roof-runner Haunt

FINAL CONVERGENCE
Makeshift Barricade

'Drink the fungus broth,' the Brewgit had said. 'What's the worst that could happen?' he'd said. The worst that could happen, as it turns out, is that you'd wake up under a vivid crimson dawn on the streets of Carngrad, the biggest runt camp to be found in the Bloodwind Spoil. Your head is throbbing, and you're fairly certain that not all of the gore coating you is your own.

You don't remember how you got here, or why the city is in a greater state of anarchy than usual – something to do with a statue of the spiky humies' king and a bucket of squig dung – but it doesn't matter. You just need to get out before your warband ends up in a fight that even you can't win. Fortunately, the winding maze of streets gives you a chance to escape relatively intact. So long as you don't get distracted along the way, that is…

D3	ARTEFACT OF POWER
1	**Supply of Blood Grog:** *This viscous liquid tastes a little funny, but it certainly provides a potent rush of energy when ingested.* Once per battle, the bearer can use the 'Onslaught' ability without needing or using any ability dice.
2	**Desecrated Flag:** *You pilfered this flag from the tower of some humie boss and now wear it as a badge of honour, much to the delight of your lads.* Add 1 to the value of abilities used by visible friendly fighters (to a maximum of 6) while they are within 6" of the bearer.
3	**Best Boss Hat:** *This imposing horned helm is surely fit for only the bossiest of bosses.* If the bearer is included in your warband, you begin the battle with 1 additional wild dice.

D3	COMMAND TRAIT
1	**Nowhere to Hide:** *This warrior loves nothing more than rooting out enemies from places of supposed safety.* Enemy fighters cannot receive the benefit of cover when they are targeted by an attack action made by this fighter.
2	**Terrible Show-off:** *If this warrior accomplishes a suitably impressive deed, everyone – friends and enemies alike – is sure to know about it.* Roll a dice each time an enemy fighter is taken down by an attack action made by this fighter. On a 4+, you gain 1 additional wild dice at the start of the next hero phase this battle.
3	**Idiot Savant:** *This warrior is not known for planning things to any great degree, but somehow their impulsive actions always seem to come good in the end.* Add 3 to the value of abilities used by this fighter (to a maximum of 6).

FIRST CONVERGENCE: A BRAWL AT DAWN

You definitely meant to make a beeline for the city's edge, you're sure of it. How you ended up in this run-down tavern in the blood-pit district is beyond you. It seems, however, that some of the patrons have taken offence to your warband's presence and the fight has quickly spilled out onto the streets, although you're all a little unsteady on your feet. Show your latest rivals who's boss.

BATTLEPLAN
Terrain: See map.

Deployment:
Draw a deployment card as normal.

Victory:
Cut Off the Head

Twist:
Eager for the Fight

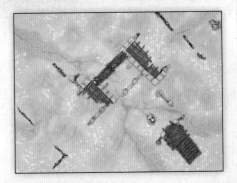

SECOND CONVERGENCE: KING OF THE CASTLE

Your escape was going well; freedom was almost in your grasp. That was until you noticed a bunch of sneaky gits hanging about on top of the shambolic roofs of Carngrad. For some reason, the sight of them lording it over you from up above has filled you with an unstoppable anger. Climb to the city's upper levels and send your enemies back down to earth. Permanently.

BATTLEPLAN
Terrain: See map.

Deployment: Draw a deployment card as normal.

Victory: Higher Ground

Twist: No Holding Back

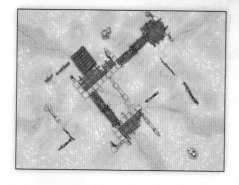

FINAL CONVERGENCE: CITY ESCAPE

No more mucking about now; it's time to get out of here before all of the city is on your tail and baying for your blood. As you near the outskirts of Carngrad, it seems your troubles aren't quite over yet. A spiked barricade blocks your path, enemy warriors circling around to harry you and pick off your boyz from the flanks. But you don't go around problems – you go straight through them. Remind your adversaries of that fact.

BATTLEPLAN
Terrain: See map.

Deployment: Frontal Assault

The Aspirant warband uses the blue deployment points.

Victory: The Gauntlet

The Aspirant warband is the defender.

Twist: No Respite

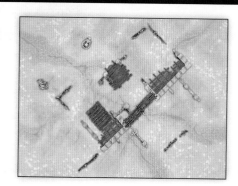

CAMPAIGN OUTCOME

If the Aspirant warband is the winner, they complete this campaign quest. Read the text below, and then choose either **Honour** or **Glory**.

With the roars and howls of your enemies ringing in your ears, you smash your way through the hastily erected barricade and make a dash for the ramshackle outskirts of Carngrad. Once you're there, you're certain you can disappear back into the wilds relatively easily – it's hard to tell where the city really begins and ends anyway, but that's the spiky gitz for you. You've already got plans forming for what you'll do once you've escaped: first on the agenda is finding the Brewgit who got you into this mess and force-feeding him his own potions. Maybe that'll teach him a lesson.

Your dreams of revenge are interrupted as an agonised holler rings out from behind you. One of your lads has been speared clean through the back of the calf by a hurled javelin; the impact has thoroughly incapacitated them, and the projectile is stuck fast in their tough flesh. You wouldn't care under most circumstances, but this warrior in particular is one of your oldest mates – you've been through plenty together, and that's just since this whole escapade began. Glorious escape is almost within reach, but can you really bring yourself to abandon your wounded warrior?

HONOUR
If you choose Honour, turn to page 54 to see the outcome and claim your reward.

GLORY
If you choose Glory, turn to page 55 to see the outcome and claim your reward.

THE WISDOM OF WOZGOBBA

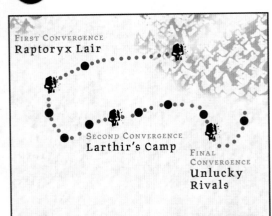

FIRST CONVERGENCE
Raptoryx Lair

SECOND CONVERGENCE
Larthir's Camp

FINAL CONVERGENCE
Unlucky Rivals

While kicking over a shanty town out in the wastes, you were approached by a muttering orruk shaman shuffling out from the gloom. Introducing himself as Wozgobba, this spell-flinger asked for your help in getting together the necessary items to perform a mighty ritual. Though there was something suspicious about the limping figure, your reverence for almighty Gorkamorka compelled you to hear the mystic out.

Wozgobba is too volatile and infirm to acquire these items himself; at least, this is his excuse for sitting around in his mountainous lair and leaving you to do all the hard labour. Should you help him, however, he promises you greater power than ever before. It's not as if you have anything better to be doing – besides, you're curious to see what this ritual's all about anyway.

D3	ARTEFACT OF POWER
1	**Raptoryx-feather Headdress:** *One who wears this impressive headdress is said to gain the speed and power of the savage Raptoryx.* Add 1 to the Move characteristic of the bearer.
2	**Da Godrock:** *This strangely glowing rock looks like Gork. Or maybe Mork. It's hard to tell.* If the bearer is included in your warband, at the start of the hero phase of the first battle round, roll a dice. On a 1-3, add 1 to the Toughness characteristic of the bearer until the end of the battle. On a 4+, you gain 1 additional wild dice.
3	**Beast-bone Cleaver:** *This crude bone cleaver is said to be animated by the most savage of predatory spirits.* Add 1 to the Attacks characteristic of attack actions made by the bearer that have a Range characteristic of 3 or less.

D3	COMMAND TRAIT
1	**Master Forager:** *This warrior seems to be inordinately lucky when it comes to finding treasures hidden in the wild.* If this fighter is included in your warband, you can make 1 additional search roll on the lesser artefacts table (Core Book, pg 68-69) during the aftermath sequence of each campaign battle.
2	**Fight Another Day:** *This warrior has no qualms about using their mates as living shields.* Each time this fighter is targeted by an attack action, roll a dice. On a 4+, you can pick a friendly fighter within 1" of this fighter to be the target of that attack action instead. That fighter is treated as being within range of the weapon being used.
3	**Loves What He Does:** *The thoroughness with which this warrior savages their prey is quite unsettling.* Add 3 to the damage points allocated by critical hits from attack actions made by this fighter that have a Range characteristic of 3 or less.

FIRST CONVERGENCE: A WILD HUNT

Wozgobba's first big request is for the fresh brains of fifty Raptoryx. The feathery blighters seem to get everywhere, so finding a supply shouldn't be a problem. You soon track down a flock of the avian creatures, only to find another warband on their trail in the beast-haunted wilds. Fight off the foul predators that inhabit this region and deal with these unexpected rivals.

BATTLEPLAN
Terrain: See map.

Deployment:
Draw a deployment card as normal.

Victory: No Quarter

Twist:
Hidden Predators

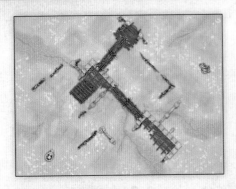

SECOND CONVERGENCE: A BAD DAY FOR LARTHIR

Now Wozgobba's asked you to fetch him the lumpen heart of an elder Jabberslythe. You're not too sure about seeking out one of these maddening beasts, but perhaps you don't have to. Forced to flee Carngrad after a banquet gone awry, the Chaos champion Larthir the Gorged has established a great feast-camp in the wilderness nearby. Perhaps you should pay his expansive larders a visit...

BATTLEPLAN
Terrain: See map.

Deployment:
Defiant Stand

The Aspirant warband uses the red deployment points.

Victory: Defend the Find

The Aspirant warband is the attacker.

Twist: The Aspirant player picks 1 twist card to be in play.

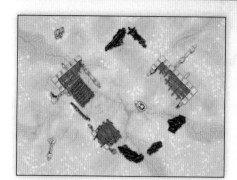

FINAL CONVERGENCE: LAST ORDERS

You're starting to grow a bit sick of Wozgobba's demands. You still haven't seen any evidence of this ritual actually progressing, aside from the orruk's occasional mumbled assurances. At least this latest request sounds somewhat magical: the shaman has sent you to recover a lockbox that is currently in the possession of a particular warband leader. Surely, there must be something magicky contained within?

BATTLEPLAN
Terrain: See map.

Deployment:
Draw a deployment card as normal.

Victory: Assassinate

The Aspirant warband is the attacker.

Twist: Dead of Night

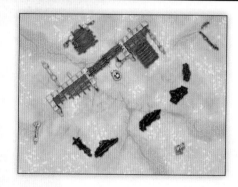

CAMPAIGN OUTCOME

If the Aspirant warband is the winner, they complete this campaign quest. Read the text below, and then choose either **Honour** or **Glory**.

While your boyz finish smashing up the last of the enemy warband and rooting around in their possessions, you recover the lockbox from their leader's corpse. Curiosity overwhelms you. Surely, after all your work, one little peek can't hurt? Upon opening the box, your brow furrows; contained inside is a glass flask, cracked and faded but still intact. Unstopping the vial, you let some of the liquid within drip onto your tongue. It soon brings another scowl to your face – ancestral duardin brew, the kind you've looted plenty of times before. Potent, without a doubt, but nothing magical.

Realisation hits you in a flash. Wozgobba isn't collecting ingredients for any kind of ritual; he's just using you to fetch him a wide array of new foodstuffs to sample. You dislike being played at the best of times, never more so than when the culprit is some uppity spell-flinging git. Some of your lads want to march back to Wozgobba's lair and confront the shaman outright, face to face. That would certainly be the 'proper', honourable thing to do, you have to admit. Alternatively, the more gittish members of your warband have some skill with brewing potions and broths themselves. Maybe you could use your newly recovered prize to prepare a little surprise for old Wozgobba...

HONOUR	**GLORY**
If you choose Honour, turn to page 54 to see the outcome and claim your reward.	If you choose Glory, turn to page 55 to see the outcome and claim your reward.

CHAINS OF IRON

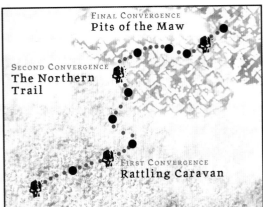

FINAL CONVERGENCE
Pits of the Maw

SECOND CONVERGENCE
The Northern Trail

FIRST CONVERGENCE
Rattling Caravan

The spiky humies have some funny ideas about things, but in many ways they are agreeable. They believe that the strong survive and the weak perish – though, admittedly, some of them have strange notions of what constitutes strength – and most of the time, they can be trusted to offer a good fight. The relationship between them and the children of Destruction is often fractious, but on occasion, deals can be reached.

You have been contacted by Graxus Kraw, an influential Iron Golem Dominar, to hunt an ogor bandit that has been seen near Golem territory. Kraw believes that your natural instincts may help you to track down the creature. Do this, he claims, and he will forge a new blade in your honour. You could do with a new toothpick – and, after all, it's just one ogor.

D3	ARTEFACT OF POWER
1	**Carving Blade:** *Though finer and more precise than your normal choice of weapon, you admit that this blade is dead good at chopping up foes.* Add 2 to the Strength characteristic of attack actions made by the bearer that have a Range characteristic of 3 or less.
2	**The Savage Crown:** *This crude amber crown radiates waves of bestial energy, sending nearby monsters into an utter frenzy.* If the bearer is included in your warband, you automatically pass bestial intellect rolls when you activate a chaotic beast within 6" of the bearer.
3	**Beast-soul Idol:** *The bearer of this simplistic but magically potent idol can unleash truly ear-splitting howls of fury.* Once per battle, the bearer can use this artefact as an action. If they do so, subtract 1 from the Attacks characteristic of attack actions made by enemy fighters while they are within 12" of the bearer.

D3	COMMAND TRAIT
1	**A Proper Brainbox:** *This warrior is practically a genius by the standards of their race. Some say they can even count to double-digit figures.* If this fighter is included in your warband, you begin the battle with 1 additional wild dice.
2	**Guts and Glory:** *Even the most fearsome of battles won't stop this warrior from wolfing down messily carved chunks of enemy flesh to restore their health.* Each time an enemy fighter is taken down within 1" of this fighter, you can remove D6 damage points allocated to this fighter.
3	**Seeing Red:** *The more wounds this warrior takes, the angrier they get – which never ends well for anyone nearby.* While this fighter has 5 or more damage points allocated to them, add 2 to the damage points allocated by each hit and critical hit from attack actions made by this fighter that have a Range characteristic of 3 or less.

FIRST CONVERGENCE: MYSTERY MEAT

Knowing ogors, the first thing on your quarry's mind will be food. Rancid caravans of flesh and bone roam the Bloodwind Spoil, trading sustenance for weapons, warriors and darker favours. You manage to corner one such caravan as it rattles through the wastes, but as you approach, the guards draw their blades and bellow a challenge. Time to put them in their place and extract the information you need.

BATTLEPLAN
Terrain: See map.

Deployment:
Draw a deployment card as normal.

Victory: The Raid

The Aspirant warband is the attacker.

Twist:
Eager for the Fight

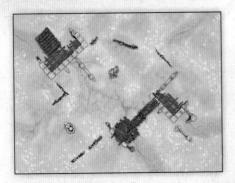

SECOND CONVERGENCE: ON THE TRAIL

From the caravan's masters, you learn of a raiding ogor who seems to be following a northbound trail. You even have a name: Dromak. It appears you aren't alone in the pursuit, however, for other warbands hired by Kraw are closing in on Dromak. You're determined to be the one who claims the prize – slip past these rivals and bludgeon them if they try any funny business.

BATTLEPLAN
Terrain: See map.

Deployment:
Frontal Assault

The Aspirant warband uses the blue deployment points.

Victory: The Gauntlet

The Aspirant warband is the defender.

Twist: Dead of Night

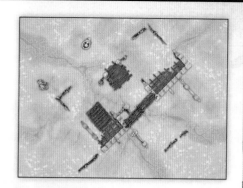

FINAL CONVERGENCE: BROKEN BONDS

Your pursuit of Dromak has led you closer to the industrial forge-labyrinth of Varanthax's Maw. Here, twisted smokestacks pump filth into the air, and the clash of hammer on warped steel echoes constantly. As you pass through a ruined forge-temple, you and your strongest lads are set upon by a band of sellswords wielding heavy iron chains. No doubt they intend to bind you into servitude and sell you on; you must escape before that can happen.

BATTLEPLAN
Terrain: See map.

Deployment:
Show of Strength

The Aspirant warband uses the blue deployment points.

Victory: No Mercy

Twist: Draw a twist card as normal.

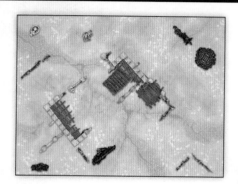

CAMPAIGN OUTCOME

If the Aspirant warband is the winner, they complete this campaign quest. Read the text below, and then choose either **Honour** or **Glory**.

As the cries of the slavers echo in the distance, you feel a presence watching you. Scavenged metal armour clanks and scrapes together as the hulking form of Dromak emerges from the shadows of a rocky bluff. You draw your weapons, ready for a fight, but the wandering ogor does not seem interested in battling it out with you. To your surprise, he instead bids you follow him towards a vast pit situated a short distance to the east. Curious in spite of yourself, you go after Dromak, helping to swiftly dispose of any guards who attempt to block your path.

As you descend into the cavernous depths, you realise why Dromak has travelled to this place. The pit resounds with the muffled roar of what seems to be hundreds of chained ogor slaves, clad in heavy iron and driven mad by hunger. The walls are marked with the portcullis symbol of the Iron Golem; you had heard that these Chaos boyz were in the business of enslaving ogors, but the sheer scale of the practice is nevertheless greater than you could ever have guessed. Gesturing to the broken manacle around his own leg, Dromak demands you help him to overcome the guards and free his kin. You could argue that might makes right, choose to incapacitate the ogor and earn yourself both glory and a fancy new blade, or you could side with him and let loose the vengeful slaves.

HONOUR
If you choose Honour, turn to page 54 to see the outcome and claim your reward.

GLORY
If you choose Glory, turn to page 55 to see the outcome and claim your reward.

AT THEIR OWN GAME

You've heard about the fighting pits of the humie city of Carngrad. The bloody sands of these arenas echo to the sound of bone-crunching, spine-shattering, muscle-tearing violence night and day – and you want in on the action. After all, no stinking softflesh is better than you, no matter how many spikes they strap onto their armour or how many heads – or lack thereof – their gods have.

It is not unheard of for the wild warriors of Destruction to enter these fighting pits, but it is uncommon. That's never stopped you before, however. When you and your mob arrive in Carngrad, it's with some refreshingly simple goals in mind: duff up as many pathetic humie 'champions' as you can, earn the attention of the baying crowds and prove that you're the toughest, meanest bunch of lads around.

D3	ARTEFACT OF POWER
1	**Da Wollopa:** *Although this stonewrought club is far from elegant, it certainly gets the job done.* If the Strength characteristic of an attack action made by the bearer is higher than the target's Toughness characteristic, that attack action scores a critical hit on a 5+.
2	**Unfortunate Mascot:** *The bearer has claimed the severed head of a former rival as a symbol of their personal prowess.* Subtract 1 from the value of abilities used by enemy fighters (to a minimum of 1) while they are within 9" of the bearer.
3	**Squigbone Torc:** *The wearer of this strange artefact can clear great distances with a single leap.* The bearer can use the following ability: [Double] Bounding Leap: This fighter can fly as part of the next move action they make this activation.

D3	COMMAND TRAIT
1	**Innovative:** *This warrior comes up with all manner of ways to shame and bludgeon their hapless foes.* Once per battle, when this fighter uses an ability, the value of that ability can be changed to 6.
2	**Notorious Bully:** *Should they meet a warband of equal worth, this warrior will strive all the harder to intimidate their foes through violence.* Add 1 to the Attacks characteristic of attack actions made by this fighter that have a Range characteristic of 3 or less. If all warbands in the battle have the same number of dominated territories, add 2 to the Attacks characteristic instead.
3	**Lone Wolf:** *This warrior is at their best when all alone, surrounded by foes.* The 'Desperate Last Stand' rule (Core Book, pg 40) applies to this fighter while there are no friendly fighters within 3" of them and there are any enemy fighters within 3" of them.

FIRST CONVERGENCE: AN EARLY RETIREMENT

For the tribes of Destruction, the path to power is simple: give your former boss a good stabbing. Whether that's in the front or the back is largely a personal choice. With this philosophy in mind, you track down a renowned pit fighter and his warriors as they carouse through the pleasure houses of the northern run-offs one night. Time to show these gits that there's a new boss in town.

BATTLEPLAN
Terrain: See map.

Deployment: Defiant Stand

The Aspirant warband uses the red deployment points.

Victory: Assassinate

The Aspirant warband is the attacker.

Twist: Dead of Night

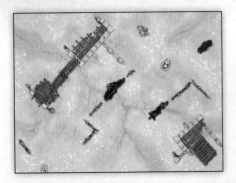

SECOND CONVERGENCE: FLIGHT AND FIGHT

You've certainly got the attention of the pit masters now. For this latest bout, they have devised something special: the arena is dominated by a central tower, and gargoyle-faced pipes mounted to the walls slowly pump in an endless stream of acidic bile. If you linger, you will be consumed – you must claim the upper levels of the fighting arena and ensure your opponents take the fall instead.

BATTLEPLAN
Terrain: See map.

Deployment:
Frontal Assault

The Aspirant warband uses the blue deployment points.

Victory:
Vantage Point

Twist: No Respite

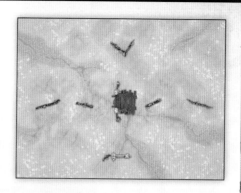

FINAL CONVERGENCE: ARMED TO THE TEETH

Your successes have made you a fixture on the Carngrad arena circuit, much to the displeasure of your fellow gladiators. It seems that they are not alone in their sentiments, and you are beginning to believe that someone wants you dead. More than usual, at least. This latest fight is further evidence of that: your opponents are clutching fine blades that have clearly been gifted by a wealthy ally. No matter, crushing them will be all the more satisfying as a result.

BATTLEPLAN
Terrain: See map.

Deployment:
Show of Strength

The Aspirant warband uses the blue deployment points.

Victory: No Mercy

Twist: Battle Frenzy

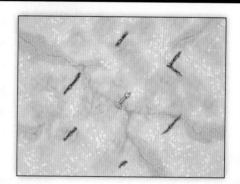

CAMPAIGN OUTCOME

If the Aspirant warband is the winner, they complete this campaign quest. Read the text below, and then choose either **Honour** or **Glory**.

Your last opponent chokes and gags, blood gushing from their lips. Twisting your blade, you watch with amusement as they convulse before letting them collapse into a broken heap. So much for all their fancy swords. Taking your leave of the arena to the baying of the crowds, you are accosted by a band of heavily armed warriors. One of them steps forward to deliver a message from their master, a powerful gladiatorial patron in Carngrad.

Apparently, your storming success in the pits has disrupted the balance of power between the various gangs in thrall to this pit lord. However, in recognition of your impressive skill and the popularity you have achieved with the masses, he wishes to offer you a deal rather than turning straight to violence. Should you voluntarily quit Carngrad and allow things to return to normal, you will receive a gift worthy of a glorious champion. It is a tempting offer, for your wild blood calls out for you to move on to battles new. Still, that same warrior spirit takes umbrage at being threatened out of your rightful inheritance. The warriors before you shuffle nervously, clearly uncomfortable with the prospect of having to face you, but should you refuse their terms, worthier challengers will no doubt come. Will you accept this offer of amnesty and claim your prize, or will you fight on regardless?

HONOUR
If you choose Honour, turn to page 54 to see the outcome and claim your reward.

GLORY
If you choose Glory, turn to page 55 to see the outcome and claim your reward.

SPOILS OF VICTORY

Through battle and bloodshed, you and your warband have emerged triumphant. Across the Bloodwind Spoil lie the broken remains of your foes, their ambition no match for your cunning and skill at arms. Whether you will cleave to an honourable path or risk damning yourself in pursuit of greater glory is up to you to decide…

Here, you will find conclusions for each of the fated quests provided in this book. If you chose the path to Honour, you will find your reward on this page. If you chose the path to Glory, your reward awaits on the page opposite.

HONOUR

A LONG NIGHT IN CARNGRAD – NO ONE LEFT BEHIND

With a grumble, you turn about and charge back into the storm of projectiles. Barbed spears and sharpened darts slice your flesh, but you do not relent. Quickly reaching your mate's side, you hoist them up and make a break for the edge of the city. It is a close-run thing, but spurred on by adrenaline, you manage to shake off the worst of the pursuit. Your freedom seems assured, and you've earned yourself some fancy new scars in the process.

EXALTED COMMAND TRAIT
Scarred and Bloodied: *No matter what happens, no matter the scrapes they get into, this warrior always comes out tougher and meaner than ever before.*

Until the end of the battle, each time an enemy fighter is taken down by an attack action made by this fighter, add 1 to the Toughness characteristic of this fighter and remove D3 damage points allocated to this fighter.

THE WISDOM OF WOZGOBBA – BLOWING YOUR TOP

Marching back to Wozgobba's lair, you demand he explain himself. The Weirdboy is outraged and prepares to unleash a storm of green sorcery. Unfortunately for Wozgobba, letting you do all the work has left him rather out of practice. Eyes bulging, Wozgobba detonates in a burst of roiling energy. You only just manage to duck into cover, though the tingling Waaagh! energy that marks the shaman's passing clings to you quite determinedly.

EXALTED COMMAND TRAIT
Glowy Green Aura: *The wild magic that surrounds you crackles and pops irritatingly, but it nevertheless offers you a deep reserve of feral power.*

Add 5 to the Wounds characteristic of this fighter. In addition, add 1 to the Toughness characteristic of this fighter.

CHAINS OF IRON – OFF THE CHAIN

Together, your warband and Dromak manage to fight your way past the slave-pit guards, break down the gates and shatter the great chains. Suddenly freed, the starving ogors pour out of the cavern and into the outskirts of Varanthax's Maw, ready to unleash primal violence until death claims them. It is certainly a more worthy end than slaving for the Golem – and, admittedly, being a liberator feels somewhat satisfying.

EXALTED COMMAND TRAIT
Topple the Mighty: *This warrior loves nothing more than putting worthy enemies in their place.*

Add 2 to the Attacks and Strength characteristics of attack actions made by this fighter that have a Range characteristic of 3 or less and that target an enemy fighter with the **Leader** runemark (☼) or the **Gargantuan** runemark (🐾).

AT THEIR OWN GAME – OVER YOUR DEAD BODY

No runty little humie in a runty little city is going to tell you where you can and cannot fight. You explain this to the armoured herald before commanding your lads to stick him good. The other warriors flee at that, doubtless intending to bring word of your actions to their master. You have made an enemy today, you can be sure of that. Still, what is life without a little risk now and again?

EXALTED COMMAND TRAIT
Brutish Bravado: *This warrior's raw self-belief is a potent weapon in its own right.*

Once per battle, this fighter can use this command trait to make a bonus move action or a bonus attack action.

GLORY

A LONG NIGHT IN CARNGRAD – PARTING SHOT

If your mate didn't want to get left behind, he shouldn't have been stabbed through the back of the leg by a sharpened projectile. That's just common knowledge amongst the tribes of Destruction. Besides, his prized weapon has skidded over towards you, and saving that is practically the same thing anyway, in your eyes. Ignoring the way your fellow warrior howls in rage and curses you for a coward, you leave his wounded form and focus on escaping yourself. Out here, after all, only the strong survive.

ARTEFACT OF POWER
Blade of the True Boss: *Claimed through opportunity, this blade is best served when sunk into the back of an oblivious enemy – especially if they're busy duffing up one of your mates.*

Add 2 to the Attacks and Strength characteristics of attack actions made by the bearer that have a Range characteristic of 3 or less while the bearer is within 1" of a friendly fighter.

THE WISDOM OF WOZGOBBA – DOWN THE WRONG HOLE

Wozgobba is pleased when you return with the lockbox, claiming that the 'magic potion' will help him access the magic needed for his ritual. He still seems pleased as he chugs down the duardin brew – and all the other ingredients you added to the mixture, whether you knew what they were or not. The Weirdboy sits back with a grunt of satisfaction; a toothy grin is still etched on his features as he keels over backwards. You decide to give him a good cooking all the same, just to make sure he's stone dead. Never can be too sure with spell-flingers.

ARTEFACT OF POWER
Wozgobba's Staff: *Wozgobba doesn't seem to mind you taking his magicking stick. It can make a truly impressive explosion, if you focus enough.*

The bearer can use the following ability:

[Quad] Mighty Detonation: Pick a visible enemy fighter within 12" of this fighter and roll a dice. Allocate D6 damage points to each fighter within a number of inches of that fighter equal to the dice roll. Roll a dice for each.

CHAINS OF IRON – RULES OF NATURE

If these ogors didn't want to be slaves, they shouldn't have let themselves be captured in the first place. You tell Dromak this, shortly before you and your warband set upon the lone ogor and wrestle him into submission. He will soon rejoin his kin in the slave pits below. Sure enough, a few weeks later, a messenger reaches you bearing an impressively choppy blade: a gift from Kraw for services rendered and a token of grudging thanks from the Iron Golem.

ARTEFACT OF POWER
The Golem's Regard: *This well-honed blade is satisfyingly choppy, especially when turned against the frail and the weak.*

Add 2 to the damage points allocated by each hit and critical hit from attack actions made by the bearer that have a Range characteristic of 3 or less and that target an enemy fighter with a Wounds characteristic of 10 or less.

AT THEIR OWN GAME – KNOW WHEN TO FOLD THEM

You're done with this stinking place. You never liked Carngrad anyway. Besides, the avaricious side of you is a little curious to know what this prize is all about. The herald – seemingly a little relieved – calls forth another warrior, who presents you with a full-faced helmet sculpted in the image of a roaring Rocktusk Prowler. It isn't exactly your style, but with a few extra combat scars and a coat of warpaint added for good measure, it'll look nice and proper – and it'll probably impress everyone back home a good amount, too.

ARTEFACT OF POWER
Rocktusk Warhelm: *This snarling helmet is dead impressive, and the more you wear it, the more you seem to have in common with the ferocious beasts whose image it apes.*

Add 5 to the Wounds characteristic of the bearer. In addition, add 1 to the Move characteristic of the bearer.

CHALLENGE BATTLES

On occasion, warbands will be called upon to undertake truly mighty tests of skill. These challenges are never easy, but the rewards – and glory – that stem from victory can provide a key edge in battles to come.

This section introduces a type of campaign battle referred to as a **challenge battle**. Challenge battles are unique battles available to any warband currently embarked upon any campaign quest. In this section, you will find 6 challenge battles for your Destruction warbands to attempt.

HOW TO PLAY A CHALLENGE BATTLE

When you challenge an opponent to a campaign battle, if both players agree, you can instead choose to play a challenge battle.

In a challenge battle, one player, known as the **Challenger**, is attempting to overcome the challenge that has been set. This player's warband is referred to as the **Challenger warband**.

The other player, known as the **Adversary**, is attempting to thwart the Challenger. Rather than controlling their own warband, the Adversary instead controls fighters that are referred to as **adversaries**.

First, decide which challenge battle you will play, which player will be the Challenger and which player will be the Adversary.

Each challenge battle has 4 sections: **Set-up**, **Special Rules**, **Battleplan** and **The Spoils**.

SET-UP

The Set-up section of a challenge battle details how the players muster their warbands. The Challenger and the Adversary will have different rules they must follow.

In a challenge battle, dominated territories do not grant additional points to a warband and glory points cannot be spent on reinforcements.

ADVERSARIES

The Adversary will have a unique pool of fighters to choose from in each challenge battle. This may be a single large monster or a group of fighters using fighter cards from existing factions. In either case, the fighters controlled by the Adversary are never drawn from their warband roster, even if the same fighter card is used.

Adversaries do not have any destiny levels, artefacts or command traits unless it is specifically stated otherwise. In the aftermath sequence, the Adversary does not make injury rolls for these fighters, nor do they roll for destiny levels for them.

THE PREREQUISITE AND THE STAKE

Every challenge battle has a **prerequisite** and a **stake**. The prerequisite is the required number of dominated territories the Challenger warband must have. If the Challenger warband does not meet the prerequisite, the challenge battle cannot be played.

If the Challenger warband loses the challenge battle, they immediately lose a number of dominated territories equal to the stake. This represents the repercussions that the warband faces in the wake of their failure and the time they must spend recuperating their resources.

SPECIAL RULES

Challenge battles may have 1 or more **special rules**. These can be rules that apply to some or all fighters – akin to twists – or rules that alter the core rules for generating a battle.

BATTLEPLAN

The Battleplan section of each challenge battle explains how to generate the battleplan.

THE SPOILS

Each challenge battle has 1 or more **spoils**. If the Challenger warband wins the challenge battle, they receive 1 of the spoils of that challenge battle. In some cases, they may receive bonus spoils for completing a specific task.

TREASURE HOARD

One of the spoils of each challenge battle is the treasure hoard. If the Challenger picks this reward, they can make up to 3 additional search rolls on the lesser artefacts table (Core Book, pg 68-69) during the aftermath sequence of the battle.

ARTEFACTS OF POWER

Some spoils grant an artefact of power to be given to one of the fighters in the Challenger warband. An artefact of power can only be given to a fighter if no other fighters in the same warband bear the same artefact of power.

MONSTERS

Some spoils will let you add the monster adversary to your warband roster. If you choose such a reward, use the rules on pages 6-8.

THE AFTERMATH SEQUENCE

After each challenge battle, resolve the aftermath sequence (Core Book, pg 66-70) with the following amendments:

- Players do not receive glory points for playing a challenge battle.

- Injury rolls and destiny rolls are not made for adversaries.

- Neither player advances on their campaign progress tracker.

Note that both players can make 1 search roll on the lesser artefacts table as normal. When the Adversary does so, they must pick a fighter from one of their warbands that is embarked on a campaign quest to receive the lesser artefact.

PLAYING AGAIN

You can play through the same challenge battle as many times as you wish, even if you have already achieved victory. Note that certain spoils, such as artefacts of power, are limited to one per warband roster.

The Narrative of Challenge Battles

Challenge battles allow players to explore the Eightpoints in more ways than ever before. You and your warband might end up trying to get a brainless but belligerent troggoth to smash up the shanty-city of Carngrad, or you might (no doubt grudgingly) defend a grot Brewgit as they cook up a potent fungal potion. You might even get into a brawl with a hulking Megaboss and claim his favourite choppa as a reward!

These battles offer their own unique challenge and are suitable for up-and-coming warbands as well as those that have completed a campaign quest and are yet to embark on a new one. For such warbands, challenge battles offer a set of difficult trials to overcome and a checklist of achievements to complete.

If you are looking to add a monster to your warband through a challenge battle, it is expected that you will first collect and paint the model yourself before challenging a friend. You then get the chance to tame the wild monster and later add it to your warband roster, while your opponent gets the chance to run amok through your warband with a very dangerous beast!

Many of these challenge battles are designed to be very difficult for the Challenger, and completing all of them is something to boast about! It will require all your tactical cunning – and often an abundance of artefacts of power and destiny levels – to emerge victorious.

Good luck, and may the gods be on your side!

A RIGHT OLD MESS

It had all been going so well. You and your lads had been poking around inside one of the great fiery dungeons that lie beneath the Eightpoints; only when you ran into a wandering mob of angry stunties did things start to go wrong. In the midst of the fighting, one of the stunties' fire-botherers had tried to use his magic – or whatever it is. As it turns out, the corrupted flames of the Eightpoints didn't appreciate that much.

Now the entire cavern is coming down around you. A deep rumble fills the air as great chunks of rock flatten any unfortunate enough to linger beneath them. There's only one way out, and to get to it means fighting through duardin as eager to escape as you are. Every moment you waste might be your last. Still, now you have double the reason to kick the stunties' heads in.

SET-UP

Prerequisite: 2 dominated territories

Stake: 1 dominated territory

THE WARBANDS
The Challenger and the Adversary each muster a warband as described in the core rules (Core Book, pg 36), with the following amendments:

1. The Challenger must muster a Destruction warband, and all fighters in the Challenger warband must be chosen from the Challenger's warband roster.

2. All adversaries must have the **Fyreslayers** faction runemark (🔥).

3. The combined points value of the fighters in each warband cannot exceed 1,250.

SPECIAL RULES

Dungeon Battle: This battle is a dungeon battle. It uses the rules for dungeon battles and the battleplan cards found in *Warcry: Catacombs*. The map dictates where dungeon terrain is set up.

Falling Rubble: Roll a dice each time a fighter is picked to activate. On a 1, that fighter is struck by falling rubble. Allocate D6 damage points to that fighter.

Note that a fighter that is waiting will be rolled for twice in total. These are the perils of standing in the same place for too long!

BATTLEPLAN

Terrain: See map.

Deployment: Into the Breach

The Challenger uses the blue deployment points.

Victory: Breakout

The Challenger is the defender.

Twist: Suffocating Heat

THE SPOILS

If the Challenger wins the battle, they can choose 1 of the following spoils:

Treasure Hoard: See page 57.

Artefact of Power: The Challenger can give 1 fighter in their warband the following artefact of power:

Super Glowy Golden Rune: *The fire stunties were fighting particularly hard to keep this glowy item out of your hands. You can see why: just touching it fills you with a wild berserker strength.*

The bearer can use the following ability once per battle:

[Double] Activate the Rune: This fighter makes a bonus attack action that has a Range characteristic of 3 or less.

GARGANTUAN CARNAGE

Gargants who end up in the Eightpoints tend to go a little bit 'funny'. Even those not obviously warped in body develop a lust for violence that is impressive even by the standards of their belligerent kind. Still, gargants often find common cause with the savage worshippers of Gorkamorka, though they cannot help but look down on those they consider little 'uns.

You have encountered one such gargant causing a ruckus in the Demnos Lowlands. Over a barrel of looted grog, you bet the brute that you could slay more enemies than even one of Behemat's spawn. It was a challenge that the gargant could hardly refuse, and come morning, he stomped off towards a ruin full of unquiet bone-rattlers, hollering at the top of his voice and daring them to come out and fight. There's no going back now – you must fight for your life and impress upon your towering rival just how 'ard you really are.

SET-UP

Prerequisite: 2 dominated territories

Stake: 1 dominated territory

THE ADVERSARY WARBAND
The Adversary musters a warband that consists of the following adversary:

- 1 Aleguzzler Gargant (pg 9)

THE CHALLENGER WARBAND
The Challenger musters a warband as described in the core rules (Core Book, pg 36), with the following amendments:

1. The Challenger must muster a Destruction warband, and all fighters in the Challenger warband must be chosen from the Challenger's warband roster.

2. The combined points value of the fighters in the Challenger warband cannot exceed 1,100.

BATTLEPLAN

Terrain: Draw 3 terrain cards; the Adversary picks 1 of them to be in play.

Deployment: The Challenger picks 1 of the battlefield edges and deploys all of their fighters wholly within 3" of it. The Adversary then sets up their Aleguzzler Gargant wholly within 3" of the same battlefield edge.

Victory: Keep a tally of the number of fighters taken down by attack actions and abilities used by the Aleguzzler Gargant and the number of fighters taken down by attack actions and abilities used by the fighters in the Challenger warband.

The battle ends after 5 battle rounds. At the end of the battle, the player with the highest tally wins.

Twist: Dusk

SPECIAL RULES

Battle Groups: The rules for battle groups are not used in this battle.

The Gargant's Challenge: In this battle, the fighters in the Challenger warband and the adversary treat each other as friendly fighters.

The Undead: At the start of the first battle round, before the hero phase begins, the Challenger must set up fighters with a Death faction runemark and a combined points value of between 950 and 1,000 on the battlefield. The fighters must be set up within 6" of the centre of the battlefield.

If the players have access to the *Tome of Champions 2019*, the fighters set up must have the **Restless Undead** faction runemark (🕱). Otherwise, any fighter with a Death faction runemark can be set up, but these fighters can only use abilities that do not require a specific faction runemark.

In both cases, these fighters are subject to the Territorial Predators and Bestial Intellects rules in the same way as a chaotic beast.

Drunken Courage: Subtract 2 from the damage points allocated by each hit and critical hit (to a minimum of 1) from attack actions that target the Aleguzzler Gargant.

THE SPOILS

If the Challenger wins the battle, they can choose 1 of the following spoils:

Treasure Hoard: See page 57.

Monster: The Aleguzzler Gargant can be added to the Challenger's warband roster (pg 6-9).

THE BIG CARNGRAD BASH

When Drosus Allslaughter, the newest Talon of Carngrad, swore to wipe out the savage beasts of Destruction that roamed the Bloodwind Spoil, he made things personal. You are still convinced that your plan was a good one. Fighting your way into one of the city's blood pits, you released an imprisoned Dankhold Troggoth. With its help, you had planned to knock down a monument Allslaughter has recently erected to his own glory.

Unfortunately, the troggoth seems to think differently. In fact, it doesn't seem to think at all. All the excitement has confused the brute and left it even more erratic than normal. More than once, it has wandered off to smash a nearby tower, sit on an unlucky foe or simply stand around drooling. You must get the troggoth moving again to reach the monument. Or, at the very least, make sure it bites off the enemy's heads rather than your own.

SET-UP

Prerequisite: 2 dominated territories

Stake: 1 dominated territory

THE WARBANDS
The Challenger and the Adversary each muster a warband as described in the core rules (Core Book, pg 36), with the following amendments:

1. The Challenger must muster a Destruction warband, and all fighters in the Challenger warband must be chosen from the Challenger's warband roster.

2. The Challenger warband also includes 1 Dankhold Troggoth (pg 10). This fighter is treated as a monster. It costs points just like any other fighter but is not added to the Challenger's warband roster.

3. All adversaries must have the same Chaos faction runemark.

4. The combined points value of the fighters in each warband cannot exceed 1,250.

BATTLEPLAN

Terrain: The Challenger places 1 building in the centre of the battlefield to be the monument. We recommend the Bell Tower, but any building no wider than 6" across at its widest point is suitable. The Challenger then sets up the rest of the terrain.

Deployment: Frontal Assault

The Adversary decides how to orientate the deployment card with the battlefield and chooses which player will use the red deployment points and which player will use the blue deployment points.

Victory: If the monument is destroyed (see right), the battle ends and the Challenger wins. Otherwise, at the end of the fifth battle round, the battle ends and the Adversary wins.

Twist: No Holding Back

SPECIAL RULES

The Monument: Fighters in the Challenger warband can make attack actions that target the monument while they are within 3" of the monument and more than 3" from any adversaries.

The monument has a Toughness characteristic of 5 and a Wounds characteristic of 50. When 50 damage points have been allocated to the monument, it is destroyed.

Puny Intellect: At the start of each combat phase, before the player who has the initiative picks which player will take the first turn, the Challenger must take a stupidity test for the Dankhold Troggoth. To do so, the Challenger must roll a dice and consult the table below.

D6	Effect
1	***Who's da bad guy again?:*** Until the end of the battle round, the Dankhold Troggoth is controlled by the Adversary. It is treated as a fighter in the Adversary warband for that battle round and is no longer treated as a fighter in the Challenger warband.
2	***Hurr hurr, the sky looks pretty…:*** The Dankhold Troggoth cannot be picked to activate this battle round.
3+	***Okay boss, let's go smash!:*** The Dankhold Troggoth activates as normal.

THE SPOILS

If the Challenger wins the battle, they can choose 1 of the following spoils:

Treasure Hoard: See page 57.

Monster: The Dankhold Troggoth can be added to the Challenger's warband roster (pg 6-10).

KRUSHED

Krusha Murgg, Krusha Murgg – he's all your lads ever want to talk about nowadays, that orruk boss who claims to be uniting the mobs of the Bloodwind Spoil. Normally, you wouldn't be against getting together for some good, old-fashioned violence, but you're sick of hearing Murgg's name. Especially since the warlord keeps sending his lads to try to 'rekroot' you. All of those swaggering messengers have ended up pummelled, shanked or otherwise disposed of for bothering you, but that's hardly the point.

Now Krusha has run out of patience. The Megaboss and his toughest lads have arrived to batter you into submission; it's time to teach him a lesson. Other members of Murgg's mob have gathered to watch the ensuing scrap. If you can impress them with suitably grisly acts of carnage delivered to their mates, Murgg will lose face – before you do him in for good, that is.

SET-UP

Prerequisite: 4 dominated territories

Stake: 1 dominated territory

THE WARBANDS

The Challenger and the Adversary each muster a warband as described in the core rules (Core Book, pg 36), with the following amendments:

1. The Challenger must muster a Destruction warband, and all fighters in the Challenger warband must be chosen from the Challenger's warband roster.

2. All adversaries must have the **Ironjawz** faction runemark (🐗).

3. The Adversary warband must include 1 Orruk Megaboss as the leader (referred to as Krusha during this battle).

4. The combined points value of the fighters in each warband cannot exceed 1,250.

SPECIAL RULES

Leave It to Da Bosses: Only fighters with the **Leader** runemark (☀) can use abilities or make attack actions that target an enemy fighter with the **Leader** runemark (☀).

A Proper Show-off: Each time a fighter is taken down, the attacking player rolls a dice. On a 4+, they receive 1 additional wild dice at the start of the next battle round.

BATTLEPLAN

Terrain: Draw 3 terrain cards; the Challenger picks 1 of them to be in play.

Deployment: Defiant Stand

The Challenger uses the blue deployment points.

Victory: Cut Off the Head

Twist: Bitter Rivals

THE SPOILS

If the Challenger wins the battle, they can choose 1 of the following spoils:

Treasure Hoard: See page 57.

Artefact of Power: The Challenger can give 1 fighter in their warband the following artefact of power:

> **Krusha's Cleaver:** *Krusha by name, krusha by nature – that was how the Megaboss described himself. Not that it mattered much in the end. Still, there's no denying that this choppa makes a particularly satisfying sound when crunching flesh and bone.*
>
> Add 1 to the Attacks and Strength characteristics of attack actions made by the bearer that have a Range characteristic of 3 or less.

PICKING YOUR POISON

On your travels across the Bloodwind Spoil, you've caught wind of a monstrous eight-legged horror preying on warbands and slave caravans. This beast strikes from nowhere, overwhelming hastily erected defences before disappearing just as swiftly. As a veteran hunter of monsters yourself, you have a suspicion as to the culprit's identity: a Skitterstrand Arachnarok, a deadly ambush predator that can tear holes in the skin of reality itself.

Though common sense suggests that hunting such a beast would be the height of madness, you decide to give it a go anyway. After all, many of the Chaos boyz here have some kind of godly blessing, which is basically cheating, and the potent venom of a Skitterstrand would even the odds. Reaching the site of the monster's last attack, you start searching around for any clues as to its location. All the while, eight malevolent eyes watch you from the gloom…

SET-UP

Prerequisite: 2 dominated territories

Stake: 1 dominated territory

THE ADVERSARY WARBAND
The Adversary musters a warband that consists of the following adversary:

- 1 Skitterstrand Arachnarok (pg 9)

THE CHALLENGER WARBAND
The Challenger musters a warband as described in the core rules (Core Book, pg 36), with the following amendments:

1. The Challenger must muster a Destruction warband, and all fighters in the Challenger warband must be chosen from the Challenger's warband roster.

2. The combined points value of the fighters in the Challenger warband cannot exceed 3 times the points value of the adversary in the Adversary warband.

SPECIAL RULES

Battle Groups: The Challenger warband must be split into battle groups as normal. The adversary is not placed in a battle group.

Deployment: The Challenger sets up all their battle groups first. The Adversary then picks 1 of their deployment points and sets up the adversary as normal.

Where Did It Go?: Once per battle, the Skitterstrand Arachnarok can use this ability as an action if it is more than 3" from any enemy fighters. If it does so, remove the Skitterstrand Arachnarok from the battlefield; it is now in reserve. In the reserve phase of the next battle round, it can be set up again anywhere on the battlefield more than 5" from any enemy fighters.

BATTLEPLAN

Terrain: Draw 3 terrain cards; the Adversary picks 1 of them to be in play.

Deployment: Draw a deployment card as normal.

Victory: A player wins the battle as soon as every fighter in their opponent's warband is taken down.

Twist: Dead of Night

THE SPOILS

If the Challenger wins the battle, they can choose 1 of the following spoils:

Treasure Hoard: See page 57.

Monster: The Skitterstrand Arachnarok can be added to the Challenger's warband roster (pg 6-9).

BLOODBATHS AND BREWGITS

You haven't had anything proper to drink in days. If you hadn't been fortunate enough to encounter the grot Brewgit Snotsnork, you might well have lost your temper, which would not have ended well for anyone. It's a lucky break for Snotsnork too: you've promised that, should he prepare a sufficiently hearty brew, you won't beat the living daylights out of him. Probably. It seems fair deal for all parties, at least in your opinion.

While some of your warband stays behind to guard the Brewgit, others have been sent to gather the ingredients. However, drawn by the curious scent emanating from Snotsnork's cauldron, a rival warband has shown up to steal the brew. In doing so, they have cut the foragers off from the guards. The ingredients must be delivered with all haste while the rest of you make sure that Snotsnork survives long enough to hold up his end of the bargain.

SET-UP

Prerequisite: 3 dominated territories

Stake: 1 dominated territory

THE WARBANDS
The Challenger and the Adversary each muster a warband as described in the core rules (Core Book, pg 36), with the following amendments:

1. The Challenger must muster a Destruction warband, and all fighters in the Challenger warband must be chosen from the Challenger's warband roster.

2. The Challenger warband also includes 1 Brewgit (referred to as Snotsnork during this battle). This fighter is treated as an ally. It costs points just like any other fighter but is not added to the Challenger's warband roster.

3. All adversaries must have the same faction runemark.

4. The combined points value of the fighters in the Challenger warband cannot exceed 1,250.

5. The combined points value of the adversaries in the Adversary warband cannot exceed 1,300.

BATTLEPLAN

Terrain: Draw 3 terrain cards; the Challenger picks 1 of them to be in play.

Deployment: Hold Out

The Challenger uses the red deployment points.

Victory: If Snotsnork is taken down, the battle ends and the Adversary wins. Otherwise, at the end of a battle round, if the concoction has been brewed (see opposite), the battle ends and the Challenger wins.

Twist: Eager for the Fight

SPECIAL RULES

Battle Groups: The Challenger must have at least 3 fighters in their Dagger and at least 3 fighters in their Shield.

The Potent Brew: At the start of the hero phase of the first battle round, the Challenger rolls two D3s. The first result is the number of snozzlewart Snotsnork needs. The second result is the number of scuttlefungus Snotsnork needs.

All fighters in the Challenger's Dagger are said to be holding the ingredient snozzlewart, and all fighters in the Challenger's Shield are said to be holding the ingredient scuttlefungus.

If a fighter from either the Challenger's Dagger or Shield finishes a move action within 1" of Snotsnork, they give their ingredient to him. Keep track of the number of each ingredient Snotsnork is given.

At the end of a battle round, if Snotsnork has been given the needed number of each ingredient, his concoction has been brewed.

Dat's a Lot of Smoke!: No ability or attack action can be used to target Snotsnork from more than 3" away this battle. This represents the billowing smoke coming from the Brewgit's cauldron.

THE SPOILS

If the Challenger wins the battle, they can choose 1 of the following spoils:

Treasure Hoard: See page 57.

Artefact of Power: The Challenger can give 1 fighter in their warband the following artefact of power:

Da Snotsnork Speshul: *All sorts of funny-coloured smoke left the Brewgit's cauldron as he worked, and he might have chucked in some of the enemy's remains to taste. Still, Snotsnork promises his brew can offer all sorts of bonuses with no side effects. Probably.*

Each time the bearer makes a wait action, roll a dice. On a 1, allocate D3 damage points to the bearer. On a 2+, pick either the Move, Toughness or Wounds characteristic of the bearer. Add D3 to that characteristic until the end of the battle.

WARCRY WARBAND ROSTER

WARBAND NAME

WARBAND ORIGIN | PLAYER NAME

CAMPAIGN QUEST

GLORY POINTS

DOMINATED TERRITORY

CAMPAIGN PROGRESS TRACKER

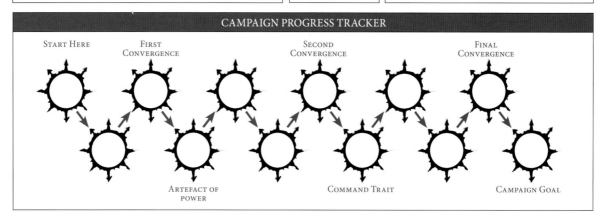

START HERE   FIRST CONVERGENCE   SECOND CONVERGENCE   FINAL CONVERGENCE

ARTEFACT OF POWER   COMMAND TRAIT   CAMPAIGN GOAL

MONSTER

FIGHTER NAME	FIGHTER TYPE	DESTINY LEVELS
		☼ ☼ ☼

HEROES AND ALLIES

FIGHTER NAME	FIGHTER TYPE	ARTEFACTS	DESTINY LEVELS
			☼ ☼ ☼
			☼ ☼ ☼
			☼ ☼ ☼